Live Stress-Free
with
Statistics and Numbers

Live Stress-Free

with

Statistics and Numbers

Dr. Vasant D. Chapnerkar

iUniverse, Inc.
Bloomington

Live Stress-Free with Statistics and Numbers

iUniverse books may be ordered through booksellers or by contacting:

iUniverse
1663 Liberty Drive
Bloomington, IN 47403
www.iuniverse.com
1-800-Authors (1-800-288-4677)

ISBN: 978-1-4759-9025-6 (sc)
ISBN: 978-1-4759-9027-0 (hc)
ISBN: 978-1-4759-9026-3 (ebk)

Library of Congress Control Number: 2013908958

Printed in the United States of America

iUniverse rev. date: 05/29/2013

ACKNOWLEDGMENTS

I would like to express my gratitude to the many people who saw me through this book; to all those who provided support, talked things over, read, wrote, offered comments, allowed me to quote their remarks and assisted in the editing, proofreading and design.

Specifically, I would like to acknowledge my mother who gave me the training to be a good person for the first twelve years of my life, before she passed away. I always think of her and appreciate the parental guidance she gave me to accomplish what I have in my life.

Also, I would like to acknowledge my wife, **Sushila Chapnerkar**, who came to US on her own in 1956, when very few Indian women did. She gave me three amazing children and gave up the option to go back to India to become the Prime Minster of India. Instead of pursuing her own career, she stayed home and raised our children and grandchildren. She gave them the parental guidance they needed to have successful lives, just like my mother did.

Because we are such a close family, all my children (**Sheila Boyington, Asha Vaidya and Sudhir Chapnerkar**), my son-in-laws (Dane Boyington and Shekhar Vaidya and daughter-in-law (Lisa Chapnerkar) and five grandchildren (Priya, Nisha, Poonam, Kalpana, and Dinesh) always been an inspiration for me. I would like to express my love and gratitude to them; for their understanding and endless love, always.

A special thank goes to my very close friend, **Asha Deshpande**, who has encouraged me to write this book since 1977. She always gave me good advice and reviewed my manuscript many times.

PREFACE

For over five decades I have noticed that people often state things without any basis, which is usually, an impression they may carry resulting from a single experience or even here-say. Such statements give no answers to questions that I have had during my years of work, travel and family-life. These statements are usually generalizations of things, situations, and people. What has been missing and what is missed are hard facts and statistics that substantiate even responses that are 'general' in nature.

Having done my PhD in Chemical Engineering with Statistics as minor, I have always been obsessed with numbers and I certainly saw the value in numbers and statistics. To many others, and me statistics tell a story but only a few realize that even existence is a statistic. Consider just a few very basic statements, questions and words:

- How many survived?
- How many die?
- Population
- Purchasing power
- Money spent
- Size of the House you live in
- Bank Balance
- Heartbeat
- Blood Pressure
- Time
- Degree of love
- Family
- Energy used
- Exchange rate

The list goes on and on.

There seems to be very little in life that has no number associated with it. Even I say family; there are a basic number of three that makes for a family in the traditional sense of how many people make up a family. Numbers equates time. The depth of love is often the result of how much time one may have spent together, the number of things that are shared in terms of areas of interest or commonalities and possibly even how many times love is expressed! This may sound unemotional but give it a thought and it has truth to it.

Most of the experiences I have used to illustrate in this book are based on me and my wife raising our kids without any body's help and also helping our extended family—our children's kids. So you can see we have experience in raising three kids and five grandkids. This number certainly adds to our credentials as parents and grandparents! In Florida we were voted as the Best grandparents in 2007.

I have traveled all over the world because of my business of marketing my Alkaline Paper Technology. I have been to 88 (eighty eight) countries and seen almost all of the Wonders of the World. Even my wife, children and grandchildren have traveled between 35 to 67 countries around the World. We took our children around the World in 1964 and took our grandkids around the World in 1994. This has given me a tremendous amount of information I call statistics, about the World we live in.

All people in the World want to live in peace and harmony and only few radicals are making this difficult for us. In 1956-1994, we traveled without any problems. Now you have to go through so many checkpoints, which costs us time and lot more money. At every gate there are 10-20 people to check you and your luggage, who use laundered uniforms and each of those people cost (about $100,000.00/year/person). The equipment used to scan cost almost $1,000,000.00. This is not a good use of our money, time and energy to further our living peacefully and economically. If we did not have these statistics, we would have only focused on loss of time and not necessarily of monetary losses. This is an informed observation coming from several trips in and out of various international and domestic airports besides facts gathered from researched reports in the media.

I also have many personal experiences to prove my points and you may think that I am bragging about myself. If you think like that; you are right. I have been perceived that way for years. When I started my consulting company; I chose the name as S A I International. The reason for this was that I had to use S as the first letter, since my wife's name is Sushila, my older daughter's name is Sheila and my son's name is Sudhir. You can see how the first letter had to be S. My second daughters name is Asha. So I used the letter A as the second letter. My name is Vasant and I should have used V, but, since I always brag; I decided that I should use the letter I. and hence my company was named S A I. By coincidence it is name of one of the Gods that I have been worshiping since 1943—Sai Baba.

When I talk about religion, it is not about going to temples, churches, synagogues, mosques, but believing in GOD being some omnipotent power, which is much bigger than you are. I normally go to the places of worship such as temples to have good thoughts and get rid of bad thoughts and not for GOD to give me anything. Since I am a human being; I also have desires and some times have bad thoughts. I go to the temples to clean my mind and dump all the bad statistics I have. So I am not an atheist.

You may think I am exaggerating the relevance of statistics. Read on and you will realize that even your life is full of numbers.

Chapter 1

Statistics

It is the mark of a truly intelligent person to be moved by statistics.

George Bernard Shaw

ℭℬ

Prime / Premiere . . .

Karl Pearson defined Statistics as the grammar of science.

Statistics is defined as the science and practice of developing knowledge through the use of empirical data expressed in quantitative form in **numbers.**

For example, a first time visitor from India who comes to America and sees only one white man from the population of about 320 million in America could go back to India and tell that all Americans are white. A second visitor who comes and sees one black man could go back home and tell that all Americans are black. A third visitor coming from India and seeing one white man and one black man and then going back to India could tell that 50% of Americans are white and 50% of Americans are black. Now a person like me who has been in America since a long time and seen a large number of Americans and who also looks at available statistical data from Government survey says that approximately 88% white and 12 % black. This information is more accurate because the sample size is bigger and provides better statistical information. In life, we cannot always have information on the entire population and hence we work on a statistically significant sample size.

This reminds me of an interesting story, that when I came to New York for the first time in 1956, I went to Gainesville, Florida by the Greyhound bus. When the bus made its first stop in Washington D.C, I had to go to the restroom. When I approached the entrance doors to the toilet for men's bathroom I saw two entrances, a sign on one showed WHITE and the other BLACK. I looked at my skin color and it was neither as WHITE as White American nor BLACK as Black American. It was in between and I did not know what to do. How was I to determine which entrance to go into?

An individual's statistics of every person is derived from the five senses (Fig. 1); and hence it is the best information to make decisions in life. You know that the five senses are:

- SEE with your eyes
- HEAR with your ears
- SMELL with your nose
- TASTE with your tongue
- FEEL with your body parts

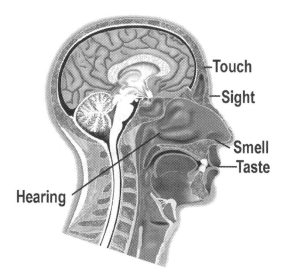

Figure 1

A person who has excellent statistical information and the knowledge to retrieve the information stored in his brain and arrives at the right conclusion is called an **intelligent** person. The person in this category stores the information in different compartments and knows which compartment the information is in when he or she needs that information to make the right decision. Recently there was a show on '60 minutes on CBS' showing six people who could tell you what the day of the week was if you gave them the date in any year. It was shown that they compartmentalize the information and retrieve it when they need it. They showed the closet of one of the persons and it showed that everything was arranged neatly.

A person who has good statistical information but does not know how to retrieve and hence comes to wrong conclusion is called a **stupid** person.

A person who does not have any significant statistical information and hence may or may not come to the correct conclusion is called an **ignorant** person. He is taking a chance to come to the conclusion.

Education, I choose to call it information or statistics, is the most important thing you can give to your kids. Education will stay with them the rest of their lives and will not be taken away by hurricane, fire like material things which we give them. When a patriot in India (Bal Gangadhar Lokamanya Tilak), was in fight with the British to leave India, all he preached was that education is the only way we can get rid of the British. He started newspapers and started the Ferguson College in Pune. He happens to be my son-in-law's great grandfather and was sent to jail by the British to Burma (now called Myanmar) in 1914 for six years, way before Mahatma Gandhi took over his ambition.

Most of the personal examples I have used depict how we as human beings use our past information to make good decisions. It is also to show how some specific instances in your life dictate your future actions.

In order to build your database of statistics in your brain, to be able to make good decisions in whatever you do, you need to be exposed to the following:

- Parental efforts and/or those of a guardian
- Education
- Travel

PERORATION

Evan Esar defines Statistics, though in a cynical way, as the science of producing unreliable facts from reliable figures, the fact remains that like everything else, Statistics can be used and misused. And if you are using it for leading a better life, you are certainly making not just good use but the best use of statistics.

ॐ

Bibliography

http://www.brainyquote.com/quotes/keywords/statistics. html#Fd93ErVQoxwX7tS0.99

Chapter 2

Information

I am disillusioned enough to know that no man's opinion on any subject is worth a damn unless backed up with enough genuine information to make him really know what he's talking about.

—H. P. Lovecraft

લ

Prime / Premiere . . .

Information is the basic determinant block that leads to the shaping of a decision. One can't overemphasize the use of information. One can only call attention to the substantial significance of appropriate information in its value and important role in arriving at results. Many a times these results change course of actions. They have known to change the course of history. False information has been known to have lead to wars. Right information has led to successful revolutions.

Results can change the path of life. Often they become life defining.

So going after the right information is an invaluable exercise, which should not be done lightly, casually or carelessly. Rather, it should be gathered with diligence and due precaution to ensure that your purpose is not negatively affected but is positively enable by—right information.

Sir Benjamin Franklin had said, "For having lived long, I have experienced many instances of being obliged, by better information or fuller consideration, to change opinions, even on important subjects, which I once thought right but found to be otherwise."

Quality of Life is based on how much information you have and the manner in which you use the information to accomplish whatever goal you have in your mind. Normally, if you think through the goal and make a detailed plan of action and attack, you have a much greater chance of achievement and accomplishment. You have to make sure that you have good statistical information. If you have bad information, what is also referred to as garbage, then you are bound to make wrong decisions, because garbage in can only give garbage out. So make sure that your source of information is reliable.

Sources of good information

Parents and/or Guardian

A child starts collecting data from the moment he or she is born. In fact, it is reported that a baby in the womb is constantly collecting information.

Hence, I believe that the environment has more to do with the progress of the individual than the genetics. I agree that genetics has to do with an individual looks, some mannerisms, diseases etc. To me, 70%-80% of the personality of an individual appears derived from the environment.

Psychologists and psychiatrists claim that 80% of the personality of the individual gets formed from the time of birth until the age of 4 years. Considering that environment has significant effect on the individual, it is critical that for the first 4 years, the child should be given the best environment. This does not mean that you ignore the child after 4 years. If you do a good job in the first four years of life, you create an envelope around the person to know what is good and bad and he or she will be able to discern what is right to do and what is wrong to do. We cannot always keep the person from being in an undesirable environment, but if the guardian of the child has consciously done a good job, it goes a long way in the building of the child's personality.

In my family, the mothers have stayed with the newborn child for at least first six years of their life, so that the child gets the best statistical information, either by parents and—equally important—by the grandparents. My wife has stayed home all the time since we were married in 1958. My older daughter began working only after her last child was six years old. Till the youngest one was four years old, she worked from home. My second daughter, who has a Ph D. in Computer Science, has been home with her kids since her first child was born in 1996 till today. She always tells me that she is planning to go at home with her children while in they are in school and then move with them when they go to college. My daughter-in-law has not worked since she is married in 1994 and has been raising her son since 2003. I always try to practice in my family what I preach.

In USA and developed countries, a woman who has given birth to a child is more prone to go back to work to preserve the family's standard of living. Then, the child is placed in the day care well before he is ready to make sound decisions on his own. The child gets the values of the babysitters. We have watched on hidden cameras in TV shows what takes place in some of these places. The children are not given the same attention that you would give them in your home.

The main reason a new mother goes to work is to maintain a higher economic standard of living with two incomes. The family can afford a bigger house, newer cars and more luxuries at the cost of not giving the child the best environment. Who can love a child more than the mother and father? One has to realize that there are more important things in life than just luxuries, at the critical time when kids are young. We have a lifetime to chase other things.

Nowadays, there are many more possibilities of working from home and hence one can work part time, while taking care of one's children.

In my case, I convinced my wife and she agreed to stay home with our kids when I moved to make a living in a small town (population of 6500) after graduating from University of Florida with a Ph. D. in Chemical Engineering. My wife, being well educated in India and USA with degrees in Law and Political Science, came to USA from

India in 1956 with aspirations to go back and become the Prime Minister of India.

During that time, unlike now, there were no opportunity to work from home and she had a hard time in adjusting to raising babies. During that time when our kids were young and the youngest was just four years old, she could only raise children and do housekeeping. This took a toll on her professional career. She even had health problems after the birth of our third child. She has never recovered completely from it. She agrees that raising children was worth the troubles that she has till today.

My two daughters and my daughter-in-law kept the tradition going, which my wife had set. However, since their field was consulting and information technology they could start working from home after their youngest kids was at least more than 5 years old. During their kids' times in kindergartens and elementary school, they averaged approximately six hours per school day of social service. In fact my second daughter, volunteered six hours per day since 1997 after her first child was born. She got a Ph.D. in Computer Science in 1991.

In India; there is a possibility of a mother going to work and leaving the child at home. In India, in the past, the families lived together as joint families. In such cases, when a child is left behind, it is taken care of by the grandmother, who has the same values as the parents.

In order to follow the tradition of grandparents taking care of the child, Indians in USA now get their parents to come to the United States to live with them and take care of children so that the mother can go to work. I think this is, in most cases, bad for the grandparents because many (I do not know how many) do not have a command over English language and cannot drive a car. Back home, they are used to having a freedom to do what they want and use public transport to go where they want. In India people visit each other a lot and it is not true in USA, where normally you have to make an appointment to visit somebody. I am reminded of a show of David Letterman, who was interviewing Aishwarya Rai, who was chosen as Miss World in 1993 in a beauty pageant. He asked her how come she (at that time was 31 years old) still stayed with her parents. She quickly answered that, like in USA, she does not have to make an appointment with her parents to see them.

When my children were planning on having kids, I requested them not to give birth to kids close to each other, so that I will not be able to spend quality time with one grandkid at a time. You can see how I succeeded. My grandkids were born in 1989, 1993, 1996, 1997 and 2002. You can see that I could be with each of my grandkids for 2 to 4 years of their life from their birth. I knew from my statistical information that the grandkids want to be entertained by their grand parents for the first 2-4 years of their lives, and then they want to go play with their friends and do not have much time for grandparents. This way I have been able to help my children in the upbringing of the grandkids, one grandchild at a time.

The grandparents coming from India call the life here, as living in a 'golden cage'. Since there are Indian television stations now and a lot more people, like them, are here, this problem is not as bad as it was few years' back. Indian grandparents have formed clubs and associations to enjoy with their peers here. In Houston, they have formed a colony close to the Hindu temple and get involved in the temple activities.

Education

Education is the best thing that you can give to your children and grandchildren. When you give education and not all the material things, only education can stay with them for the rest of their lives. The material things can be destroyed by accidents, hurricanes, storms, and decline in stock market.

I made a request to each person in my family to have at least one postgraduate degree. That is what I considered to be an educated person. Some people say that having higher degrees is not needed to be a good person. I am saying that you have to be a good person and have higher college degrees so that you have the capability to think for yourself and know where to get information to accomplish what you want to do in life. I have been to school and colleges for 23 years (actually it would have been 24 years, had I not been able to jump one grade in elementary school) and have four college degrees (including a Ph. D. in Chemical Engineering) and took courses in Management for one year.

Only bookish knowledge is not sufficient to make the appropriate decisions. One should have had exposure to extracurricular activities—some kind of sport for boys, could be baseball, football, basketball or tennis; for girls it could be basketball, tennis, dancing (ballet, jazz, tap, Indian classical—Bharat Natyam, Kathakalli). Boys and girls could also learn a foreign language, learn some musical instrument (I am presently taking lessons to play Tabla, which is Indian drums), and belong to a scholastic club (viz. public speaking, personality development). Extracurricular activities, teach more than just book knowledge, they shape your personality, make it more rounded. Ballet, for example also teaches one to stand erect. In your normal life you need not bow down to the one whom you are talking to. Bowing down is an admission of inferiority. We, in India, bow down to our elders to show respect.

Per capita income in USA of Indians, as compared with others in the USA is almost 80% higher than the national average in 1980, 1990, and 2000 census data. It is also the highest amongst all the other ethnic groups. China is second at 40% higher than the national average. I think this is because the Indians and ethnic groups put a lot of emphasis on education. In my family, I advise every member to get a Ph. D and if not a Ph. D, to get at least two Masters' degrees. My grandson went to kindergarten school in San Jose. In his school there were only ethnic groups' children and less than 5% Native Americans. This school is also very expensive and name of the school is Challenger. Still ethnic group spend their money on excellent education at not material things at that age. Since Indian parents have excellent education, they have good income (as mentioned above) and can give them material things also. When we give new cars to our children, we instruct them that if you misuse the car it will be taken away from them. Till this day we have not had any problems with, our kids and grandkids, associated with driving new cars. There is an actor in India, who ran over people sleeping in the streets of Mumbai and did not even stop to see what he had done. This is bad behavior. The material things can always be gotten later, since you will have long adulthood working career after they getting a good education.

What I have seen in USA is that the parents support their children to get an education till 12th grade, then, most of the children are told to fend for them to get a college education. Indian parents support their children till they get their first college degree. What normally happens is that the children here, when they get out of the high school, get involved with girls or boys, get married, have children and buy a house and then say that I have responsibilities so I cannot afford to go to college. Where is the necessity of getting married at 18 and living an independent life. Why not wait till one gets a college education, a good job and then get married. You have a lifetime to get married, have children and buy house, like I say there is a lifetime to acquire material goods.

My family went to eat at Bern's Steakhouse in Tampa. We let the valet park the car. When we came out of the restaurant, I gave my valet stub to the attendant and he asked me what type of car I had. I said it was a Mercedes Benz. When a US native came after me and gave his stub to the attendant to bring his car he told the attendant that his car was also a Mercedes, but it looked like a Volkswagen. He also mentioned to me that I must be an Indian Doctor, because they mostly drive a Mercedes Benz.

I have attended seminars by Zig Ziggler, who is considered an authority on the subject of memorizing. At the seminar he asked 50 people at random at the beginning of the seminar their names and when the seminar was over he could remember all the names. He says that you need to associate with something you know to recollect the information you want to remember. So, the more things you know, the more associations you can make. Of course, knowing more things comes from getting more education.

My experience is as follows:

I have a project to get all the pictures (more than 31,000) I could find since 1912 and scan them and put on a CD. I have also indexed them by year and month. Since I have been doing this for the last fifteen years, I am seeing the same pictures very often to index them and check any pictures that are not correctly indexed or not being in proper sequence. Thanks to this exercise, my entire life is mapped and recalled very vividly.

Most people do not know the keyboard on the typewriter. They can type well by knowing a, b, c, and d. It was so good that I learnt typing, shorthand, German language and ballroom dancing in India before I came to US in 1956 for graduate studies. Taking lessons in German and French in India before I came to US helped me to pass required language proficiencies. When I got my Ph. D in Chemical Engineering, it was required to have some knowledge in French and German to translate technical articles written in those languages.

Learning typing has helped me type my thesis for my M. S. and Ph.D. thesis. One of the best things is that I can use a computer quite well because, you need to know typing the fast way. Since I travel a tremendous amount internationally, many times, when I go through Paris airport, I use the computers in the Airport lounges in France and to my utter surprise I found that in France the typewriter or computer keyboard is different from any other in the World. They have a, m, @ and others in different location on their keyboard. All the countries I have visited and that are 87 countries until 2012, I have found the same keyboard like in US, except for France.

When I was coming to USA from India, I got off the ship at Marseilles. I knew very little French and I could not communicate with the local people. The French people are very proud of their country and their language and usually think that they are the best people in the World. In order to order food at the restaurants I had to show the waiter what they had served at the next table, because the waiter did not converse in English and spoke only French. I did not have a command on spoken French. Thanks to my education, I could make associations, communicate and accomplish what I needed to.

Being a professional is good for your professional development, and one has to make sure that puts best efforts to be the best in the business. It is not that easy, because people are competitive and especially professional people have a lot of jealousy. To show that you are better, you need to do research and publish technical papers. In Universities, if you are a professor then you have to deal with—*publish or perish*. I have tried to publish papers and give talks on my technology that I have been selling for the last 52 years. Now since Google has come along, most of the information you need, you can get for nothing. This has affected the people like me who consult. Ten years ago if anybody wanted to know my technology, they had to come to me and I could then consult even for very basic information because it was not available easily. Now most of the basic information is available on the web.

When I presented a technical paper on alkaline sizing with Precipitated Calcium Carbonate (PCC), which is my profession, I made some interesting observations in India. In 1993 when I presented this paper I asked the Indian Paper Industry people to start using this technology. By 2008, most of the world was using it—almost 90% and in India it was only 3%. When I presented the similar paper in 2003 (ten years later), I first showed the slide giving this lecture in 1993 and I asked the audience it is not 1993 but it is 2003 and asked, 'what have you done to convert to this technology,'—'NOTHING'. Ten years have gone by since then and Indian paper industry is still in 2008, using the old technology. Using the number of conversions all over the world vs. the numbers in India made my talk much more forceful. Finally, in 2009, first on-site PCC plant was built in India. In 2011, I presented a technical paper on manufacturing PCC at a conference in India, attended by over 30,000 people from various countries in the World. They were there to attend the largest exhibition of papermakers and suppliers of equipment and chemicals.

In India, most of the times the father does not know exactly what the kids are doing and in which grade in school they are. When we were growing up in fifties and sixties, mothers took care of the household chores including raising children and father's responsibility was to provide for his family.

To get better statistical information, computers were developed. Since now majority of the population in developed countries has access to computers, information is more easily available. The computer, again, is based on the numbers zero and one. You see how numbers are important. All operations are done using these two numbers. Normally we use base 10 for our numbering system. In 1970, schools tried to go to any base instead of base 10, but this did not last and in two years it was dropped.

With advent of computer, one can get most of the statistical information on any subject through the Internet, mostly using Google. Through more information, your association's increase, therefore your education also increases.

Since I came to US in 1956, a major development was the development of computers and software to solve problems. In 1962, after I graduated from the University of Florida, I bought the first calculator made by Sony and I paid $ 290.00 at that time. It could only add, subtract, multiply and divide. Now several companies give small calculators for free, as a souvenir, for promotion and advertisement. These not only do addition, subtraction, multiplication and division, but also have memory to make complicated operations.

Later in 1965, a computer was available in Atlanta, Georgia called Mark IV, where I had to feed a special tape, with my information put on the tape and transmitted by phone to the computer and then I would get the results of my work. It was quite cumbersome and time consuming. Then a personal computer was developed and I bought it for my daughter. It was called Commodore 64 and we still have it as an antique. From these initial beginnings you can see what has transpired in the development of computers and software. Now they are available on cell phones and I do not think that this is the end of it.

Since many people are now thinking that education is the solution to all the problems in the world, including, I think, terrorism, we are striving to find better ways to teach. For better method of teaching, there was also one new approach tried in the middle schools, when the classrooms for individual classes were changed to have four classes in the same room and four teachers taught individually in one class room. This did not last either.

In the 1970, something new was also tried in schools. The students in math class were allowed to study at their own rate. My daughter was doing seventh grade math in fourth grade. Now this system has been corrected to have AP courses in most schools to teach the gifted children.

Most of the people get their information about their own life by believing in horoscope and the signs of their birth month. Most of the time when you read in newspapers the forecast for your signs or what you get in the Chinese restaurant as Fortune cookies, it applies to any body who reads it, and almost independent of the month of their birth. There are 7,000,000,000 people in the World and if you assume that the signs are distributed evenly then in every sign there are people with the same sign. So you can see there are not 583,333,334 People with the same sign and have the same traits and I do not think it is right. My wife would exclaim dramatically, 'God forbid there are not that many people in the world like me'. Actually my preliminary survey shows that more people born with Virgo sign are much more than 583,333,334. The reason is the Baby Boom after the war. In both cases to be born with a Virgo sign, you have to be conceived nine months before, i.e. in the cold month of winter.

Travel

In order to build your database of structured statistics in your brain, you need to travel and see other events for yourself. By seeing something, you tend to remember it more than just looking at a picture. You build associations based on what you are experiencing.

There are four basic modes of travel:

1. Road—Bicycles, Motor cycles, Automobile, Bus
2. Rail—Train
3. Sea—Ship
4. Air—Airplane

Well, soon some might call Space as the fifth mode.

Bicycles, Motor cycles

Since bicycles and motorcycles are not much different now, than they were 50 years ago, except for the horsepowers of motorcycles and lower weight of bicycles, it is not necessary to discuss further.

Automobile

Since the cars came in existence since 1885, they have gone into quite a change. The cars in early 1900 had basic amenities; I am not sure if they even had a radio, leave alone air-conditioning, cruise control, and heated and cooled individual seats.

Cars have been around for a longtime and my father had the first driving school in India in 1922. We have always traveled by car, which was unusual in 1920s. Since then the automobile industry has really taken off. India now builds Mercedes, Toyota, Nissan, Honda, Chevrolet, Hyundai and many other cars.

US automobile companies are used to manufacturing many brands and each brand having many different models. For instance, if we talk about General Motors, they have had Chevrolet, Cadillac, Buick, Oldsmobile Pontiac, Saturn, Hummer and Opal. Chevrolet brand had Caprice, Impala, Bel Air, Biscayne, Malabu, Camaro, Chevelle, and Chevett. Chrysler has had Chrysler Imperial, Desoto, Dodge, Plymouth, and Jeep. Ford had Ford, Lincoln, Mercury, Fraser, Kaiser, Pinto, and Ford brand had other models like Taurus, Falcon, Fusion, and Focus.

If you look at the foreign automakers, they have two major brands

Honda has Honda and Acura
Toyota has Toyota and Lexus
Nissan has Nissan and Infinity
Hyundai has only one brand and several models.

In the last ten years General motors dropped Oldsmobile, Chrysler dropped De Soto and Plymouth. As a consequence of recent problems in the auto industry, General Motors and Chrysler have taken loan from the US government. Ford did not take any loans perhaps, because they had only three brands. Ford has now gone to only two brands after dropping Mercury like all the foreign automakers. General Motors dropped Oldsmobile some time ago and now have dropped Pontiac, Saturn, and Hummer. General motors have also closed down several factories.

We have seen that Toyota took over No.1 automaker of the World by selling more cars than General Motors, which had been on top until then.

All of us know that the automobile market for US manufacturers is very bad. Again, you can look at the number of different cars made by the biggest American car manufacturer, General Motors and that number is too large. Since I come from Automobile family in India, I am always interested in cars. Since Ford had only three brands they did not need stimulus money from the Government to manufacture cars. In fact, the share of Ford was down to $1.00 in 2009 but as of November 2010 it was $16.00. In the mean time, General Motors and Chrysler could be filling for bankruptcy and Government had to give billions of dollars to keep them alive and it still looks like they are not going to make it. Now look at Toyota, they have only two brands, Toyota and Lexus, Nissan also has two brands—Nissan and Infinity, Honda also has two brands Honda and Acura. Mercedes Benz has just one brand and so does BMW. Based on this, I am not surprised at the demise of General Motors. In 2010, all of the American car manufacturers are profitable, since they shut down plants, which were not profitable.

Since in US it cost maximum up to $ 4.00 per gallon of gas, when it comes down to $ 3.65 we think it is a bargain. We all forget that in 1956, we were paying just $0.17 per gallon. You can see that the numbers are relative and not absolute, and they seem to be good or bad based on the relative statistics or information.

We do not quit driving on the holidays because every year 42,000 +/-1000 people die on our highways. If you consider the number of people who drive man/miles; it is not statistically significant. It is claimed that the air travel is the safest mode of transportation. The problem with statistics is that if the person who died on the highway is your relative, and then even one is statistically significant. The same is true about war in Iraq, if one of the soldier died, out of approximately 4000 (Oct '08) out of 180,000 who were there, was your relative then the statistics does not apply because for your statistic, it is one out of one i.e. 100%.

Car accidents are many and that is the reason that you have to drive within the speed limits. They are based on statistical information that after 35 mph in cities it is not good, it is true for 55 mph on secondary highways and 70 mph on super highways. It is also requires that you drive behind a car with the distance of at least one car length per 10 mph, because it takes that much time to avoid accident if you have to suddenly stop. It is also known that at 55 mph the gas consumption is optimum and at higher speeds it goes down significantly. In US every year, there are 42000 +/-1000, traffic deaths on the road. It has also been found that at lower speed there are less automobile accidents.

Price of cars in India is almost double the price in dollars as compared to similar models in America. It is not only because of taxes, but is also because most of the cars now sold in India are manufactured by American, Italian, Japanese, and Korean companies. Therefore, they are mostly imports, which get taxed.

It was interesting to note in that in India, the cars are given the last priority on the roads. Pedestrians have the first right, bullock carts next, handcarts next, rickshaws next, trucks next, and buses next and last are the passenger cars. In spite of this, the passenger car owners pay most of the road taxes.

Bus

In most countries mostly town transport uses buses. Now there are more buses to go from one city to another and reasonably priced so that average person can use it. In India most of them are still not air-conditioned. There are special service buses used by tourists in most countries in the world. Almost all are air-conditioned and equipped with TV, restroom and refreshments.

Train

In USA the train service is mostly for transporting goods from one place to another. There are very few passenger trains. USA does not have high speed trains like Japan or what are being constructed in China. In US, plans are being made to build some regional passenger high speed trains to go between big cities in Florida.

In India, train is the main transport of not only goods but also passengers. India has the biggest train network in the world. Train travel is also reasonable in pricing. Now there are even double Decker trains, which are quite luxurious with air conditioning and dining cars.

Airplane

The airplane is the fastest and safest mode of transportation. There are much fewer deaths per year when traveling by plane than by car. In USA the commercial airlines reported no death in 2007, 2008, 2010 and in 2009 it was 50.

When I came for the first time to USA, I traveled by ship from Bombay to Marseilles, then traveled within Europe and came to London. From London, I took an airplane to New York. It was propeller run and took 14 hours for the journey. Since then jets are taking 6-7 hours for the same journey. In 1956, there was not much airplane traffic because it was very expensive and the only reason I flew that time was that I could not get any reservations on the ship. At that time there were no security checks. Plane hijacking wasn't an issue. Since now the airlines have to be worried about planes being hijacked, there is a lot of security. If you look at any security at the boarding gates, you see minimum of 10 security people at each gate. Each security person costs approximately $ 100,000 and they wear nicely laundered uniforms. I do not think most of us used laundered clothes everyday. The scanning machine also costs about $ 1,000,000 per piece. You can estimate how much terrorism is costing. This is definitely a waste of resources. The same amount can do wonders, if spent on development.

I was at the Paris airport on Dec 23, 2001, when the gentleman with the shoe bomb, flew out on AA flight at 9:00 am. I was supposed to board Air France flight at 8:00 am but it was cancelled and they put me on another Air France flight, which left at 10:00 am. If they had room they would have put me on the flight at 9:00 am, with the Shoe Bomber.

Since more people are flying these days, there are traffic managers in order to control the traffic in the air to avoid accidents. I was on a plane Boeing 747 in 1974, there were only eleven passengers flying on the plane, which had a seating capacity of 300 passengers. Now when you fly, almost all planes are fully occupied.

PLANNING

Planning is very beneficial.

I have always had a 25-year plan and then make short-term plans from there. The 25-year plan is actually a vision statement. From it, one makes detailed plans to accomplish your goals.

Most of the major companies, the space programs and I have a 25 year plan. This plan is divided into five-year plans and further subdivided into one-year plans. From the one-year plan one can do the detailed assignments to accomplish the plan. Tracking your plans in this way leads to success. We all want to accomplish what we plan. My track record is that when I plan anything, almost 90% of the time I accomplish my objective. We also schedule more carefully so that your chances are very high to accomplish your objective.

The Industrial Engineering program in the 50s and 60s was just involving time and motion study, basically human engineering. Now, all that has changed and plans and programs are mostly statistically oriented working in tandem, like a engineering system that deals with the creation and management of systems that integrate people, materials and energy in productive ways.

How are these productive ways determined?

Using such concepts as Operation Research, the tool used to make good management or good decisions. These are based on statistical information. Queuing Theory and related concepts were developed to predict how the products from different locations could be shipped to customers with minimum travel and cost.

PROGRAM EVALUATION REVIEW TECHNIQUE, commonly abbreviated PERT, is a statistical tool, used in project management; this is designed to analyze and represent the tasks involved in completing a given project. First developed by United States Navy in 1950s, it is commonly used in conjunction with critical path method, called CRITICAL PATH METHOD.

CRITICAL PATH METHOD, commonly abbreviated as CPM, it's an algorithm for scheduling a set of project activities. It is an important tool for effective project management. CPM is project-modeling technique developed in the late 1950s by Morgan R. Walker of DuPont and James E. Kelley, Jr. of Remington Rand. Kelly and Walker related their memories of development of CPM in 1989. Kelley attributed the term "critical path" to the developers of

Program Evaluation and Review Technique which was developed at about the same time by Booz Allen Hamilton and the US Navy.

When you try to do any job, you should be qualified to do the job. My father had a saying and I will translate that into English—*'the person who knows how to do a job should do it, if you try to do somebody else's job, of which you do not have experience, you keep on tumbling and will loose for sure. If your experience is in one field, you should not try to do work in some other field of which you do not have substantial knowledge. You are statistically bound to fail, since you do not have the education, the training to support your work, your job'*

When you plan to do anything in life you should have at least two alternatives. If the first alternative is not available then you have already thought of the next alternative. When you do this ahead of time you do it without tension, if you have to decide after the first alternative is not available you think of the second alternative under tension and the statistical information in your brain is not used smoothly.

Say, you want to go out to eat, you should first prioritize what you want to eat, and then you have to decide which restaurant you have to go. This way you save money, time and energy—the aspects of TEAM.

My wife and I were supposed to fly to India with my elder daughter's family and our plan was to fly from Tampa to New York and then to Paris and meet them in Paris, where they would come from Atlanta. After we boarded the plane in Tampa to go to New York, the pilot announced that New York airport is closed because of bad weather and the flight is cancelled. Since I had thought of the second alternative already, I got up right away and went to the ticket counter and being the first one, I could get the ticket agent and told him that there was a flight from Tampa to Cincinnati and from Cincinnati to Paris. The flight from Tampa to Cincinnati was to leave within an hour and he ticketed my wife and me and we boarded the plane and he also got my luggage redirected. This way I met my daughters' family in Paris as we had planned and then proceeded to India. If I did not have the second alternative then I would not have been able to stay on my projected plan.

If you have to make any decision, there are always three parts to the decision that has to be made. This involves **T**IME, **E**NERGY **A**ND **M**ONEY and the word is **TEAM**.

> **T** is for Time
> **E** is for Energy
> **A** is for and
> **M** is for Money

I met a salesman at Udaipur Airport in India and he had the word TEAM inscribed on his shirt. But, he had used that word in a different way, more tuned to his sales position:

> **T** is for Together
> **E** is for everyone
> **A** is for Accomplishes
> **M** is for more

In my word TEAM, it represents the three resources every one has—*Time, Energy* and *Money*. This is constantly changing in *value*. When you make any decision life, however small or large you have to consider how much you have of these resources and then make the decision. The basic concept is that *you give more of, to get what you have less of.* In old times bartering was the only way to trade. Suppose if one had 100 tomatoes and other had 100 potatoes, then they would trade 50 tomatoes for 50 potatoes.

If you look at Time, then you know that everyone in the world has 24 hours in a day. Just because you are rich or a king or a janitor, nobody gets any different amount because of his/her position. This resource, once you use, it is gone. You cannot retract it. So use it very wisely. Time will be discussed in detail in a later chapter.

When you are young, you have a lot of energy and lot of time but not much money. In such a case, you make decisions based on using all your energy and time you have to minimize the money spent. Say if you are going some place and if you go by train it will take more time and energy but you will have not to spend much money. But when you are older and you have not much energy or time and you tend to have more money, then you will go by car or fly.

Once, when I was going to the airport, I saw a sign showing that if you park in the long term parking area it will cost $ 8.00 per day, but if you park at the terminal then it will cost $ 20.00. What do you think I did when I was 78 years old and going only for 2-3 days? If you say that I parked at the terminal, you are right. I want to save energy and time also and was willing to pay the extra money. If I had the same situation when I was less than 50 years old, I would have probably parked in the remote long term parking area, since I would try to save money and have extra energy. Again, as I have said before, you have the three resources, you have to use wisely at that particular time, depending how much of each resource you have and you trade by giving up what you have more of to get what you have less of.

NUMEROLOGY

Numerology is the study of the occult meanings of and their influence on human life. It all starts with your name and birth date. They are the database from which a numerologist is able to describe you, sight unseen. Number values are assigned to the letter in your name. By adding these—with the number in your birth date—in a multitude of combinations, a numerologist establishes your key numbers. He then interprets the meaning of these key numbers, which results in a complete description of your personal characteristics.

There are eleven numbers used in constructing numerology charts. These numbers are 1, 2, 3, 4, 5, 6, 7, 8, 9, 11 and 22. Larger numbers that occur from adding the numbers in the complete birth date or from the values assigned to each name are reduced by adding the digits together until the sum achieved is one of the core numbers. One merely needs to add the components of the larger number together (repeatedly, if necessary) until a single digit (or master numbers 11 or 22) results. Each of theses number represents different characteristics and expressions.

For your name components, the alphabet is divided in 9 bunches and assigned number 1 though 9 for each group of nine letters.

This prediction is based on statistical information obtained by people who developed this system. Since now there are seven billion people in the world it is very difficult to predict behavior with these numbers. There are many things happening in lifetime now, which cannot be statistically predicted, it is almost impossible to use this technique.

This is, as mentioned earlier, is not any different from the fortune cookies which predict what is going to happen with your life. All these predictions are written in such a way that you can think that it applies to you.

Astrology is another crutch people use to explain the future. **The sign, which predicts what, is going to happen every week according the predictions printed in the newspapers also applies to anybody with any sign.** They are written in such a way that it will please people reading it as individual fate.

In India, when a child is born, a horoscope is drawn which shows the signs in a quadrant of the Horoscope, and based on this it also gives you the starting letter of the name you give to the child. **Based on this information the astrologer also determines what the profession of the child should be.** I was predicted to be a lawyer and I became an engineer. My name was supposed to start with letter U, but I was named Vasant. So you should not depend on these predictions, but use the statistical information given by your surroundings and then use the information to predict your future course of action.

When we talk of a horoscope, where did the astrologers get their data? It has to be based on the facts they have statistical data on hand for famous, average and notorious people and by looking at their lives and their signs they predict your fortune. So if somebody was born under the same sign as Mahatma Gandhi, he will be like him. It is true about the signs under which serial killers are born and if you have the same type of horoscope, astrologers predict that, that is the way they are going to be.

Some of the attractiveness of numerology and other predictions mentioned above come from the desire to find somebody who will tell you that you are full of hidden strengths and powers, and who will reinforce your deepest needs and emotions. Some people who do not have the power to think for themselves are simply waiting for somebody else to tell them what to do with their lives. How can a total stranger tell you what is going to happen to you in the future? Your own brain, which has been collecting information since your birth, should be the best one to tell you what to do. This does not mean you do not take advice from others. In fact, this advice is part of the statistical information, which is in your brain. Like I always mention, your GOD is your own BRAIN.

Dr. Vasant D. Chapnerkar

Peroration

Parental presence in every element of interaction that a child gets to experience until at least four, followed by good education and wide travel ensures that an individual has a fair amount of ability to arrive at the right decisions in life.

৪০

Bibliography

1. Information quote from
    http://www.brainyquote.com/quotes/keywords/information.html

Chapter 3

How we use our statistics and information

True genius resides in the capacity for evaluation of uncertain, hazardous, and conflicting information.

Winston Churchill

ೋ

Prime / Premiere . . .

The world today is suffering more acutely than ever because of the phenomenon of 'imperfect information'. This phenomenon occurs because while we are equipped to make choices and have the options available, often we do not have the data to base our decisions upon . . .

Knowingly or unknowingly we are pulling out data from our data bank to increase the winning probability, to have the best chance of success. Success may mean making money, saving time, or saving energy, since all these are important for our well-being.

For example, consider that you go to make a cup of tea and you go to the refrigerator to take milk and find that there is no more milk in the refrigerator. What happens next,—we make so many decisions to accomplish our outcome to bring milk for the tea.

First, you think about which brand of milk you need to buy. Since there are so many alternatives available the decision becomes more complicated. You may want to buy whole milk, 1% fat milk, 2% fat milk, skim milk, evaporated milk, and powdered milk. So go ahead decide based on your statistical information on your likes and dislikes, considering the advantages and disadvantages of each. The more knowledge you have (more education), the better decision you can make.

Second, you need to think how much it is going to cost and whether you have that much money with you or do they take credit card and do you have the credit card which the store where you are planning to buy milk.

So next, you have to decide which store you are going to. You again have too many options to consider. Do I just want to go get milk only or am I going to shop for other things and what those other things are. If you decide to buy just milk then you decide not to go to supermarket because it may be far and will take lot more time to get the milk. Of course at that point you figure out, how much extra price you will have to pay to get milk from small store close by.

Once you have decided where to go, you think about how I am going to get there. You need a car and you have to have the keys for the car and also know that the car has gas to go that distance. If you want to be silly, you also think (*sub-consciously*) that the car has good tires, and other essential parts to drive the distance. If you have more than one car, then you have to decide which car to take and you have to know which car is easy to park and that the car you want to take is parked where it is easily accessible.

Once you have decided which car to drive, you have to think about which route you will have to take to be there in shortest time and come back with the milk. Now you have to look at the time and decide which way to go depending on the least congestion on the way. This will be decided if the time is close to people going to work or coming from work. This is based on your statistical information on previous trips to that store.

You now get to the store and have to decide where to park, if the store has more than one entrance and where is the isle, which has the milk. So you get in the store and have to decide whether you need a handcart or a regular cart, depending on how many items you are going to buy. When you have gotten your items, you look for the cashier with the shortest line so that you can get out quickly.

I have a very interesting anecdote about this—several years ago, I went to shop for two items at the grocery store with my, then eleven year, granddaughter. When I saw that all the regular lines were long, I looked at the counter where you buy cigarettes and other things like that. I saw nobody was there so I told my granddaughter I will give you ten more minutes of life by going through that line. Sure enough we got out in a hurry. When I tried to brag to my granddaughter that I saved her ten minutes, she told me, "Grandpy (that is loving name for Grandfather) I was not going to stand in the line and do nothing for ten minutes, I was going to read the headlines on the magazines which were there."

Once you got your milk, you have to again decide—which is the best way to go home, to have your cup of tea.

Exhausted?? YES.

From the above discussion, you can see how many decisions one has to make just to buy milk. You are making decisions all the time about whatever you do. If you have past information well in place, which I call statistical data, you do the job in the shortest time with the least money and energy spent.

Now to discuss the information you need to accomplish any objective in life, be it going to store, buying anything, or doing anything, you have to use your knowledge. This knowledge has to be involving the use of Education, Statistics, Numbers, Economics, Science and Technology and of course you know all the above by studying it in school or college, reading, personal experiences. Since I have been to 89 countries and regularly and keenly meet people and see places, it has given me extra valuable knowledge, which I call personal experiences.

STATISTICS AND NUMBERS

Statistics is everywhere and you can either use it for you to make good decisions or you can twist to suit your point of view, which may be right for you but not for majority of the persons. As mentioned before, for statistics to be valid to make good decisions, one must have adequate sample size.

Earlier it was mentioned that numbering, along with statistical information is very important for decision-making.

Suppose you are going to have a party and you can invite only 10 people at this time and you have 100 potential invitees. What do you do is start counting 1 to 10 and for each number you are assigning a name. The one you are closest is number 1 and one whom do not like at all becomes number 100 in your selection. This is decided by the brain going through all the statistical information you have on each of the people and you rank them. In the chapter on relationships it is described in more details.

Most of the people use LUCK as something that they get when they are not expecting it. For anything to happen you have to do something, in case of lottery, you still have to go and buy a ticket to win. Winning is a statistical chance. So, I say that it is not LUCK that gets you something, but it is a statistical chance of winning and odds are against you because in any lottery there are sometimes million possibility and you have to pick the right combination and have to win with one against millions. So your chances are low and almost impossible. People always talk about being at the right place at the right time. For me, your chances are higher if you *guestimate* which is the right place.

You can know how important is statistical information when you have to go to a doctor. Now days if you have problem with the knee you have to go to knee doctor. For every part of our body functions, there is a specialist. For heart problem you go to a cardiologist, for problems with the bones and if you have to be operated, you go to orthopedic doctor. For your nervous system malfunction you go to neurologist, for problems with your urination, you go to urologist. For problems with your hearing you go to an audiologist. For problems with your eyes, you go to optometrist or ophalmologist and the list goes on . . .

Hence, after a doctor gets his general degree, they go into specialization. What is specialization? It is having more statistical information in that special field. When you spend your time in specialization you learn more about it and not much about other fields. This way, you have a lot of statistical information as to how to treat that particular defect. When you go to an orthopaedic doctor, there is one for knees, one for elbow/arms, one for neck, one for back.

This is because they have more statistical information in a small area so that they can have a lot of information on specialized subject and other areas of expertise do not dilute their information. You always go to the doctor who you are told that he is the best in that area. You also ask the doctor how many patients he has treated with that type of injury or disease; it may be cancer, heart problem, arthritis, muscular dystrophy, or multiple sclerosis.

When I was raising our kids and grandkids, I always said that you should have an engineering degree and not go for management or marketing as your bachelor's degree, the reason for this has always been that engineers think black and white, their decisions are made on facts and numbers, hence, I call it thinking BLACK AND WHITE. When you go to management and marketing, the education is based more on psychology and how to convince people to do what you want them to buy. I call that thinking GREY. In later life you know that if you learnt how to think BLACK AND WHITE, then you can play GREY, but, if you first think GREY, then it is difficult to think BLACK AND WHITE.

According to me accounting, financial, insurance companies, just play with numbers and make you decide what they want you to buy, and they make tremendous profit doing this. The ones who toil make the products they represent make very small wages. We all know that a bottle of drink you buy for 50 cents, the cost of the liquid in it costs only three pennies, if that is all. The rest of the money you pay for this product goes towards packaging, advertising and management, sales and marketing people. We know that the ones who have the most money in this country are the Insurance companies. Insurance companies, like marketing people try to convince on the fear of you dying or falling ill. Nowadays they sell insurance on missing flights, having accidents, falling ill and so on. What some people call you—insurance poor.

Things repeat themselves and if you know how then you can use that information to your advantage by following what you did then, that it worked for you:

1. Every 4 and half years Boeing 747 plane has crashed.
2. I went to Marseilles every 22 years since 1956
3. I bought a Sony TV from the same dealer every twelve years
4. In 1986 I was awarded a contract, which was not given to another company. In 2007 the same thing happened with the same company.
5. In the years, which are multiples of 20, the Presidents of USA have been either murdered or attacked.
6. When I took my family around the world in 1964, my older daughter was 30 months old and we celebrated my younger daughter's first birthday in Mumbai. Interesting past is that in 1994, I took my two granddaughters around the world,

older was 60 months old and we celebrated my younger granddaughter second birthday in Mumbai. The coincidence is that, if you observe, that when you invert 6 in 1964 it becomes 1994 and the granddaughters were twice the age of my two daughters. So you see, you have repetition of events.

7. Another interesting statistics is that I was born in India on Gokul Ashtami, and my son was born in this country on Valentine's Day, which I think is similar because both are based on being affectionate and having a lot of girl friends. I have not found my other girl friends yet, may be in next life . . .

When you go to store to buy shoes, you have to first tell them what size you want. The shopkeeper gives you the size shoe you want (depending on your gender and your individual foot size, the shopkeeper gives the size you need.) Due to much specialization, the shop also gives the option to know what width you need. Women's shoe sizes are different than men's. Now days because of specialization you also can get in different widths and styles. They are also assigned numbers to differentiate and to keep track of the inventory. This is critical to order replacements.

Nowadays with the use of computers for everything, every design of anything is based on numbers and not like it used to be—by name.

Why do we celebrate Thanksgiving and Christmas and feed meals to migrant workers, and others who need help? What do they do the rest of 363 days in the year?

It is known that when you repeat anything 21 times it becomes part of your permanent memory. So when I was going to school in India, I wanted to remember for getting good grades I used to read it many times. At that time I did not know that you need to read it 21 times to make it part of your permanent memory, or on other side it becomes part of the temporary memory and you forget it after a while. *Repetition* is the name of the game for remembering. You also know that when they play songs on the radio, they play the most popular songs every hour and less popular less often. When I was growing up, I used to stammer. Hence for me memorizing the subject by reading 21 times, got rid of my stammering, as per of my doctor's advice. I read loud and exercised my tongue so that it would become more flexible. In school, when my turn used to come in the class to read, I used to switch places so that I did not have to read, since I was conscience of my stammering and did not want to be ridiculed by my class mates.

Since both Ebbinghaus and Radoosovlljevich say about remembering, that about 40% to 50% of matter is forgotten when not repeated immediately or soon after that day. If the matter is repeated for 10 minutes just after an hour of learning it, the matter will be easily remembered for a day. If, after a day, the matter is repeated for about 4 minutes, the matter will be well remembered for a week and if a third review or repetition of about 4 minutes is given after a week, and a fourth review or repetition given about 4 minutes after a month, the matter will be lodged in the long term memory for a long time, even for life. It may need an occasional review in the months following to fix the matter still more strongly in the long-term memory for life.

To start a new company you need involvement of and proficiency in at least three different disciplines to guarantee success. If you need only one discipline, then there will be thousands of people who can do it, if you need two disciplines then there will be hundreds of people can do it, but if you need three disciplines then there would most probably the people who can do it are in single digits. Just like in statistics, there is 66% for 3 sigma, 90% for 2 sigma and 95% for a sigma.

Never find a pen to write near a phone? This does not happen only when small kids are around. I have seen that happen in many instances. When you find the pen, then it is out of ink or the ink has dried off and the pen cannot write. So whenever you may be taking notes, make sure that you have pens, which write.

In statistics, we always say that you have to have sample size large enough to represent the population. There is one exception, if you pick up only one grain of rice from cooked rice, you can say that all the grains in rice are cooked or not. This is true because when cooking rice, all the grains get the same heat. You cannot do this with any other activity, because statistically, you have to have a sample size to predict the outcome.

We all use the word **Karma**, which is defined as things happening because of your deeds. As I have emphasized in this book that it is not destiny, but it is the statistical chance for that to happen. If you win a lottery we say it is luck, but I do not call it luck because one has to go and get the lottery ticket and it has a statistical chance to be the winning number.

You can also think why certain people like some things and other like something else. It is again based on the information they have in their brain about that particular thing. Some people like sour things, some people like sweet things. It is based on their information, when in the past they ate sour or sweet things they had good experience and hence they like it. It is for the same reasons people like certain clothes to wear, cars they drive, watches they use, and houses they stay in. Some of these also depend on the affordability of the person. We all know, all use has to be affordable for that person. We also call it flattering one's ego when someone buys Rolex Watches, a Mercedes Benz, lives in a big home, and wears exclusive clothes because he/she can afford it.

Communication causes 95% of the problems; either you have not heard what one said or understood differently from what was intended for you to hear. So when you tell somebody something, you have to make sure that he/she has heard it. I always ask them to repeat what they have heard. All of us are preoccupied and one hears what one wants to hear and not what was said.

I feel that you need to spend quality time with the person you love, want to be with, instead of sending flowers and cards. This is because I do not believe in emotion and passion, which are not statistically measurable and are intangibles.

Batteries and tire are guaranteed for a certain number of years, for them to function satisfactorily. Same is true with the human heart and knees of the human body, which are good for 77 years for men and 81 years for women, as studies showed in 2010.

When you are reading any paper or magazine, you see the headings. If it is very negative, I normally do not read the article to find details. I think it is not worth keeping these details as my statistics and they would be negative influences on my thinking. Sometimes it may be better to read the negative articles so that you know what not to do. However, I generally do not do this.

I have mentioned earlier many times that if you start thinking from your heart instead of from the brain, you make decisions that are not necessarily in your best interest. This is because the heart does not have the statistical information to make good decisions. I call thinking from the heart is like passion, emotion, psychology, philosophy and does not have statistical information to make wise decisions. We know that all the information required for heart to function comes from the brain. You know when you get excited the brain realizes the situation that needs to be handled, so the brain sends information to the heart and starts pumping the blood faster. We all know how erection for men occurs because your brain knows that the person in this situation wants more blood to flow so that the desired result can occur. The main purpose of Viagra is to pump the blood faster from the heart.

Why do we have rankings? They are basically statistical information presented in a form that people can understand and use, to make informed decisions. College rankings are very important to find out how you are compared to the other colleges. The ranking system is present in Universities for each of the colleges, for each of the disciplines. These rankings are created using a rubric, assigning points to many attributes. There are many surveys done of colleges by many organizations. Just to illustrate the point I have picked the ranking done by Kiplinger's personal finance of Feb. 2008. Of course I picked this because University of Florida was ranked second in USA and I am a graduate of this university and I am also on Chemical Engineering Faculty Advisory Board. Kiplinger has used several criteria for their numbering system.

For sports rankings of college sports and professional sports is mainly based on win and loss record. However, since all colleges do not play every one in a season, another system had to be designed. Earlier, it was only Harris poll, USA Today poll, Computer poll and ESPN poll. The final championship was decided first by taking the winner of individual divisions and they competed in the Bowl games, but this still did not give the best team as the Champion, hence the BCS poll was designed. It is called Bowl Championship Series standings. In this poll you rate the colleges based on Harris poll, USA Today poll and Computer Rankings. BCS is five game arrangements for post-season college football that is managed by the 11 Football Subdivision (formerly Division 1A) conferences and Notre Dame. Its' purpose is to match the two top ranked teams in the final BCS standings in a national championship game and to create competitive match-ups in four other BCS bowl games.

Nielsen Ratings are audience measurement systems developed by Nielsen Media Research to determine the audience size and composition of television programming. Nielsen Ratings are offered in over forty countries.

The system has been updated and modified extensively since it was developed in the early 1940's by Arthur Nielsen, and has since been the primary source of audience measurement information in the television industry around the world. Television as a business makes money by selling audiences to advertising rates, schedules, and program content.

Nielsen Television Ratings are gathered by one of the two ways: by extensive use of survey, wherein viewers of various demographics are asked to keep record (called a diary) of the television programming they watch throughout the day and evening, or by the use of Set Meters, which are small devices connected to every television in selected homes. These devices gather the viewing habits of the home and transmit the information nightly to Nielsen through a "Home Unit" connected to a phone line. Set meter information allows market researchers to study television-viewing habits on a minute-to-minute basis, seeing the exact moment viewers change channels or turn off their TV. In addition to this technology, the implementation of individual viewer reporting devices (called people meters) allows the company to separate household viewing information into various demographic groups. In 2005, Nielsen began measuring the usage of digital recordings and the results indicate that time-shifted viewing will have a significant impact on television ratings. The networks are not yet figuring theses new result into their ad rates at the resistance of advertisers.

The most commonly cited Nielsen results are reported in two measurements: rating points and share, usually reported as (ratings points/share). As of August 27, 2007, there are an estimated 112.8 million television households and 249 million TV sets in the U.S. A single national ratings point represents one percent of the total number, or 1,128,000 households. Share is the percentage of television sets in use, tuned to the program. For example, Nielsen may report a show as receiving a 9.2/15 during its broadcast, meaning that on average 9.2 percent of households were tuned in at any given moment. Additionally, 15 percent of all televisions in use at the time were tuned into this program.

The Oscars: Every January, when the calendar has turned to a new year, the attention of the entertainment community and of film fans around the world turns to the upcoming Academy Awards. Oscar Fever hits, building to a crescendo in the annual presentation of golden statuettes, when hundreds of millions of cinema lovers are glued to their television set to know who will receive the highest honor in filmmaking.

All voting for Academy awards is conducted by secret ballot and tabulated by international auditing firm. The awards are given to the film or persons who get the most votes in their category. It is again another numbering system.

The Emmy Awards: These are administered by three sister organizations who focus on various sectors of television programming; the Academy of Television Arts & Sciences—prime time and daytime, sports, news and documentary and international programs. The awards are to recognize excellence within various areas of television industry. The awards symbolize peer recognition from over 15,000 members of the Academy. Each member casts a ballot for the category of competition in his or her field of expertise. It is again another numbering system.

There are many awards, local, school, college, or sports, which again number the best and rank them using numbers. The awards are given based on statistical evaluation.

Did you know, your zip code number also gives you information? Zip code is the system of postal codes used by the United States Postal Service (USPS). The letter ZIP, acronym for Zone Improvement Plan, is properly written capital letters and was chosen to suggest that the mail travels more efficiently, and therefore more quickly, when senders use the code. The basic format consists of five numerical digits. An extended Zip+4 codes include the five digits of the ZIP code, a hyphen, and four more digits that determine a more precise location than the ZIP code alone.

The first digit in the ZIP code represents a certain group of U.S. states, the second and third digits together represent a region in that group (or perhaps a large city) and the fourth and fifth digits represent a group of delivery addresses within that region. The main town in a region often gets the first ZIP codes for that region; afterward, the numerical order often follows the alphabetical order. Generally, the first three digits designate a sectional center facility, the mail-sorting and distribution center for an area.

Even credit card companies have a numerical system in use:
American Express credit cards start with number 3
Visa credit cards start with number 4
Master Card start with number 5
Discover credit cards start with number 6.

Telephone numbers are also based on the location first is the country code, then the area in the state and then the numbers, which specify the individual phone.

Each highway, county, state or federal has its own number. How are they assigned? Going north and south have odd numbers, and those going east and west has even numbers. When it is three digits for national highways then if the first digit is even, then it goes around the city and if the first digit is odd, then it is a spur and does not go around the city. The roads going around the cities are called bypass and go faster instead of going through the city, which has a lot of traffic and traffic lights.

Social security numbers, frequent flyer numbers, professional or other society members all have number specific to the person, so they can be identified and their accounts can be available to the person.

When you graduate from school or college, you have grade point average, which decides the rank in the graduating class. The valedictorian has the highest grade point average and solitarian has the next highest average. When my older daughter graduated from high school, they had to go to the third decimal point to rank the first three top students. By the old system the highest grade point average used to be 4.0. Now, since there are AP (higher level) courses are offered to smarter students, they get points over 4.0. My daughter was valedictorian of her high school class and her grade point average was 4.66 because she took high-level courses. Now I see grade points from schools as high as 8.0.

Results for elections can be predicted based on a statistically select sample, which sometimes can be only 1% of the total votes. They have studied which precincts are statistically valid as sample. Sometimes, the election results are so close that even if approximately 130,000,000 votes for national elections, the results are not final till the absentee ballots are counted and in 2000 the count in Florida took a long time to decide who the President of USA was going to be.

Since many people are investing money in the stock market, you have to keep up with what is called the Dow Average, which is a number. The Dow Jones average, the oldest continuing U.S. market index, is a way of measuring the combined stock values of 30 big U.S. companies. It started out with 12 components, including defunct companies like U.S. Leather Co. and Tennessee Coal, Iron and Railroad Co. The only original component still around is General Electric.

These days, the index has expanded to reflect the U.S. economy's move away from big industrial companies. Staples of the modern Dow include big financial companies like Citigroup Inc., technology bellwether IBM Corporation and drug manufacturer Pfizer Inc.

Charles Dow, who launched the index in 1896, originally just took the price of one share of each company's stock, added the numbers up and divided by the number of companies. The average when the index launched was 40.94—a quaint little number compared with Dow's record high of 14,165.43 on Oct. 9, 2007.

Today, Dow Jones & Co. has come up with a mathematical formula to adjust for things like stock splits or new companies being added or removed. The idea is to keep the index consistent and comparable over time. At Dow Jones this is handled by changing the divisor to a number that is divided into the total of the stock prices. This divisor currently stands at 0.122820114.

I saw an advertisement in local newspaper, advertising their sleeping mattresses with a number, they call, Sleep Number. They claim that each individual have a specific "Sleep Number" which defines your level of comfort while you are sleeping. With adjustable firmness on each side, two people can experience ideal comfort in the same bed. This way the bed has been clinically proven to relieve back pain and improve sleep quality.

The partisans of the hypotheses of the Indian origin of the numerals always create, deliberately confusion and an amalgam between the history of the Indian mathematics and the history of our modern numerals. To argue the thesis of the Indian origin of the numbers they confound voluntarily between: the "zero intuitive" of Brahmagupta: "Sunya", that means "nothing", the "number zero" used in the representation of the numbers and "the mathematical zero" defined by the modern mathematicians.

"Sirf" designate the "number zero" and "Shunya" designates the "intuitive zero", thus "Sirf" is not a tradition of "Shunya". "Sirf" does not derive, from the Indian word "Shunya" since the word "Sirf" and its derivatives existed in Arabic long before the appearance of zeros itself. The mathematical zero is represented by symbol "0".

When you are listening to songs on the radio, they also use statistics as to which songs to play more often than the others. They usually play songs most often per day, which are on the top of the chart, usually every hour. They play less often the songs on the bottom of the chart, usually once per day. The chart is again based on their statistical information, based on how many records (or CDs) they have sold.

I recently read an article in an Indian newspaper in this country about one person, who to my surprise wrote that she does not plan and does whatever she feels like it. I think statistically to find a person who can be successful like her will be very low probability. But that is why statistics in important and is not all-inclusive.

Thinking process of an individual depends on his statistical information in their brain. Normally shallow thinking people have not much statistical information so they talk about what we would call trivial information, such as how are you, what did you eat for dinner, how is the weather.

Deep thinking people, who have more information and hence talk about thinking more than what questions are given, as against the *shallow* thinking people. *Bright* thinking people, who have a lot of information and are also able to retrieve it as needed talk about futuristic things, such as what is going to take place in 5-25 years hence and how we can position ourselves to be of use to the world.

Dr. Ward C. Halstead, Professor of psychology and director of medical psychology regarding the power of memory, perception and judgment has done research.

Some of his findings are:

> Up to the age of 50, four out of five executives function mentally, as well as most 25 years old executives.

> Beyond 50, there was a slight deterioration in the 60 and 70 years old executives, but this drop in mental efficiency was so slight that it made hardly an appreciable difference among the old and the young executives.

> Earlier we considered than 40 years was over the hill. I think now that is changed to 50 or even may be 60 years, because people are living longer. People used to consider that you have not attained your life's goal by 40 you will not be able to reach it.

This is understandable when we realize that the human brain has ten billion neurons, which can store up the contents of 90 million books of 1000 pages each. The theory, we believe, that we lose brain cells continually throughout our lives, which causes serious mental decline, pales into insignificance, in this light. Apart from the fact that we can generate new connections far more rapidly than the average loss of brain cells, it can also be shown that even if we lose 10,000 brain cells a day from the time we were born, we had started with so many that the total number lost by the age of 80 would be less than 3 percent.

In some cases it is good even to have negative thinking, because at least you are using brain and not let it idle. This is especially true of older people who have dementia or confined to wheel chair or bed.

Most of the people think that India's main economy is based on call centers and Information Technology. The fact is that India's IT shares is only 3% of GDP. Rest of it is pharmaceuticals, automobiles, and entertainment.

What I seem to be getting here is how the mind works, the importance of the mind and its liking for science and logic, keeping in mind a changing world that has to do with progress built on science and the role of the mind. No emotions, in short. I think a pointer is how science, and not emotions, gets nations together. If love were all that mattered, the world would be one. Interdependence depends greatly on economics and trade and most of that comes from the use of logic and science and not the heart that might respond to form and nice things that are said. At the end of the day, if actions do not follow the said words, then nothing effectively matters or means anything to the recipient. I will go through the rest in a short while.

Exploring the neurobiology of politics, scientists have found that liberals tolerate ambiguity and conflict better than conservatives because of their brains work. Analyzing the data showed that liberals were 4.9 times more likely than conservatives to show activity in the brain circuits that deal with conflicts and were 2.2 times more likely to score in the top half of the distribution for accuracy.

Tonya Reiman, a New York based author is an expert on body language. She says that **knowing what the body is saying is a vital part of making a good impression**, because appearance determines perception. Xerox Corporation in their school for their employees teaches that for sales people the necktie is important to make the first impression. Whenever I travel to Florence Italy, where fashion ties are marketed I have bought silk, handmade ties for my son, who works for Xerox. Of course, standing straight shows confidence.

People try many different diets, exercise to reduce weight, but it is very important to know that the key to weight is in your head (brain).

Exercising regularly can make your real age as much as 9 years younger. Changing bed linens, vacuuming, dusting, scrubbing kitchen and bathroom floors is considered as physical activity, also pulling weeds, painting and folding laundry count toward the 30 minutes of exercise recommended. But doing all this with a proper mind-set is necessary.

When I was working in China there was the threat of SPARS and it was only that seven people had been affected in the southern part of

China. For me, to have only seven cases of the 1,200,000,000 people are not statistically significant. It is true of Swine flu.

A nine-year-old girl got one million dollars for inventing how to make bacon strips cook faster and without too much oil dripping out from the bacon. This gives very crisp bacon strips, without the oil attached to it. She invented a process to wrap the bacon strip on a stand, made up of a vertical and a horizontal rod to wrap the bacon strips on the rod, like we mentioned earlier about putting clothes to dry on a string to expose more area.

In this invention, she also used the theory of gravity. Normally we put bacon on paper towel and put it in microwave or oven to cook. When the oil comes out of the bacon on the bottom the towel absorbs side of the bacon, but still some of it stays attached to the bottom side of the bacon and all on the top is still attached to the topside of the bacon. There are pans designed to cook bacon and drain the oil better, but still a lot of oil still stays attached to the bacon. By using the rod to wrap bacon, she used also the center of gravity principle to drain the oil from the bacon. By wrapping on the rod the oil freely falls down the bacon strips, is discharged and does not remain attached to the bacon strip. Center of gravity means the force towards the center of gravity is pulling all matter on the earth.

In my business to market the technology to make brighter paper with greater opacity, which would not yellow, I developed the technology to use Precipitated Calcium Carbonate (PCC), especially for printing, writing and copy papers. One never sees paper, on which bible is printed, ever turning yellow. We call this permanent (alkaline) paper. Now, all over the world 90% of the papers I mentioned earlier are made using Precipitated Calcium Carbonate.

The reason why PCC is incorporated in paper as filler is to neutralize the acidic atmosphere we live in. Earlier to make paper good for printing, acid-sizing (water resistance) system was used. In that case the atmospheric acidic conditions attacked the fibers and turn them yellow. Since I use PCC in my technology in the paper, the PCC neutralizes the atmospheric acidic conditions and leaves the fibers alone and hence they do not yellow.

Another thing that PCC does to paper is introducing air in the paper. The PCC filled paper has 67% air, while paper made in acidic conditions and clay filled paper has only 35% air. When you introduce air, you create a lot of air/filler, air/paper interfaces. The advantage of having these interfaces is that they reflect back the light falling on them and hence the paper has better hiding power. By hiding power I mean that it is more opaque and you cannot see what is printed on the backside of the paper. It also makes paper lighter and hence you save fiber, which is approximately three times more expensive and hence the paper can be made cheaper. I have been selling this technology all over the world since 1961.

This principle of making opaque look is also present in the waves you see in the ocean and also your water faucet, which sucks in air. The air present gives the multiple air/water interfaces and the water looks white. The waves look white because of presence of air.

How rolling bags were invented to save time and energy?

When you are not holding the bag in your hand you do not have to bear all the weight of the bag. The rollers on the bag take most of the load and what you do is mostly direct which direction you want to go. Since you are not using your energy to carry or hold the bag you can go faster, as fast as you can walk since you do not have the weight of the bag to carry. The rolling wheels are also good if they are larger and can run smoothly, having less friction and hence lower energy.

ECONOMICS:

We all know what is happening to the cost of medical care. There are four parties in this business—doctors, insurance companies, lawyers and hospitals. Most of us have heard horror stories that some patients in the hospitals are charged 5-25 dollars for a pill of Tylenol or a similar drug. All the above parties mentioned above say that they charge more because the other charges more first.

We all know that there are no free lunches. Whatever you do, you pay for it. I am always annoyed when motels advertise that children live and eat for free. Actually what they need to say is that this is included in the rate you pay for the room. Would they let children come by themselves without their parents paying for the room and live and eat free?—Of course, not! I do not think that if the kids come by themselves they can eat free. What they really mean when you pay for your room you has already paid for the kids eating (this is an incentive). So actually the kids do not eat free. This is actually a gimmick of marketing. We all know the marketing people advertise the products on the TV, newspapers and magazines create the need for the product they are advertising and then you go and buy it, whether you need or not.

Have you wondered why supermarket prices often end in 99 cents?

It is a marketing gimmick to price goods at 99 cents, instead of 1 dollar, 9.99 instead of 10 and 99.99 instead of 100 dollars. This is done so that it is less than 1 or 10 or 100 dollars and makes the buyer feel better about spending.

In an interview with the Daily Telegraph, "undercover economist" T M Hartford explains, 'why retailers know what they are doing when they slap that bright orange sticker on a cereal box.'

To change the most money without losing customers with price hike, they go to the sweetest price point there is—99 cents.

Here why Hartford says, it works:

They make change. "Product prices with 99p endings are difficult to pay for with exact money," says Hartford, a good thing since "the sale must be recorded to open the register" and "the shop cannot just hand over the product and steal the cash".

The 'left digit' effect. This "suggests that consumers cannot be bothered to read all the way to the end of a price." Hartford says "$

79.99 reads as '70 something dollars.' The alternative theory is that a price ending in 99 cents is simply shorthand for good value"

It is better than ' 4'. Hartford points to field experiments from 2003 in which a mail order company switched around its advertised prices. "A $59 dress would sometimes be priced at $54 or $64 instead," he says, and prices ending in '0' were more likely to find buyers, relative to the prices ending in '4." That said, people might simply ignore the pennies and round down.

Viewing the advertising on TV is also interesting, when you find that the manufacturers of drugs convey messages that ask consumers—'to go to your doctor and ask him to prescribe their drug'. I thought that is why you go to the doctor—for him to tell it to you and not you telling him.

It is also interesting to note that marketing has several gimmicks. One of them is to reduce the size of the packet and sell at the same price. Then after some time bring back the original size and increase the price making you fell that you are getting a bargain.

Since the price of gas has gone up so much, it is now apparent it will help with fuel efficiency to lower the speed limit. It has been calculated that if you drive at 55 miles/hr you can save gas (approximately 10%), but it takes longer time to drive say 100 miles—1 hr. 49 minutes. while at 70 miles/hr it takes 1 hr and 26 minutes so you save 23 minutes. We all want to save time but this costs also more for gas, if you assume the price of gas as $ 4.00/ gal and your car give you 25 miles / gal you can save 0.4 gallon of gas and $ 1.60. Again going back to basics, if you have time you will drive slower, but if you are in a hurry (which most of us are) we do not mind to drive at 70 miles/hr. In the month of June 2008, the Americans drove 10 billions of miles less than in June 2007, mostly because of the higher price of gas. You are seeing also the sales of SUV and big cars have slowed down and smaller cars and hybrid cars are more in demand. Many are talking about buying scooters for short distance travel. I always felt that big SUV's, which were designed to drive on rough roads in the forests, were being used to take children to school and go grocery shopping. When the economy was booming you saw more SUV's in the market than minivans. Before minivans there were station wagons. I make my own statistical survey when I am driving on the highway by counting SUV's, minivans and station wagons. Before 1970 only cars and station wagons were available. They introduced more station wagons than passenger cars. Now station wagons are extremely rare. When minivans were available in the 70s you started seeing as much as 3 times more minivans than station-wagons and in the 90s you started seeing three times more SUV's than minivans. Since the price of gasoline in 2007 started getting higher (towards $4.00 per gallon), you started seeing four times more minivans than SUV's. Now you rarely see big SUV's like Hummer, Escalade from Cadillac and Navigator from Ford.

How do you count success? Most of the people equate success with material wealth. Some call themselves successful if they have done good things in life, again the problem is what qualifies to be good deed. Most people will call Mother Teresa as successful.

We normally look for how much wealth people have. Generally it is done by what is the square footage of a man's house, what kind of car he drives, what kind of watch he uses, what kind of brand name clothes people wear and what brand of shoes he wears. All can be deduced to $ in US, Rupees in India, Rubles in Russia, Pounds in England and so on . . .

Whoever said that money cannot buy love got it woefully wrong for it seems that being financially sound is of the prime requirements for men these days. A survey in UK has found that only men who earn 35,000 pounds a year,—about 10,000 pounds more than the national average of 22,248 pounds are considered a "catch" by women, and have a better statistical chance of settling down and passing on their genes.

In a poll of 1250 people, 66% said that they would prefer a partner who earned more than the national average, rather than one with a better sense of humor, looks, or a higher IQ. As of now, people judge whether another person is well off or not on first impressions, it seems that the best indicator is a Surrey accent, as per 77%. The false sun-tan acquired by visiting parlors is not going to fool people, for only, 1% of those questioned associated it with being wealthy.

Can money buy happiness?

Yes says "RealAge" article. We know that sounds like you have heads screwed backwards, but, it is true. You can buy happiness, if you know what boosts your pleasure.

Actually we could say that lack of money brings unhappiness.

With material goods, even after you have bought them, you keep on comparison shopping. Discover you could have gotten it cheaper or there's a cooler version coming soon, and good bye happiness, hello buy's remorse. But, if you are well economically you can forget about this misery and go on with your life thinking that you got that at fair priced when you made the decesion to buy it.

If you are a very happy person and you go to buy a car, what will the dealer tell you "give me money then only I will sell you the car". Everyone's level of what they call happiness is different. Some people are happy with minimum money required for bare existence, but, most of us want a lot of a more, like nice house to live, good clothes to wear, good car to drive and good food to eat. Indians want a lot of money so that send their children to get the best education. All of us need as much as$60,000.00 per year for each child for college education. One cannot provide that unless you earn that kind of money.

In our family our kids and grandkids have been to private schools and recognized colleges. Where my grandkids have been to kindergarten and the fees were $ 25000 per year per child. In such kindergarten almost all were Indian or Asian and just one American born kids out of 21 kids in the class.

The point I am trying to make is that you have to have excellent education and hence you to have that income. Education is the most essential part of being a good citizen and do only good things in life to make a better nation where you live.

Bhagwat Gita tells us that you have to give yourselves totally to GOD and be in his service. Only Priests, Yogi's can do that. Gita also preaches not to expect any rewards for the service you do. This not possible in the World, where we have to have food, clothes etc to live, then who is able to buy when you do not earn money. Finally I have gotten several Yogi's, who come from India, to correct and say that about 5-10% of the time you devote to GOD and use rest of the time to earn money to pay for our expanding material needs.

Casual clothes and not formals also seem to be another indication, as nearly half of the people polled said that they would wear jeans, T-shirts and trainers if their income crossed the 100,000 pounds mark. Only 7 % said that a suit indicated wealth. The survey was carried out for a new television show, 'Payday', on five. It is also known that if you dress better you feel better. Marketing specialists say that the most important thing that you wear for a sales call or important meeting is to use the best necktie.

Alex Menzies, a deputy commissioning editor with Five, said that a poll showed that wealth, more than any other quality is what will get men the women of their dreams. Wealth is now the biggest motivator for love, though it's tricky to know who's got a big piggy bank or empty wallet.

Brain has logic or statistics but the heart does not have any logic since its job is to pump blood to all parts of the body. You always should think with the brain and not with the heart. Heart has passion and could end you in trouble, but not if you use the brain.

Why do we wrap gifts? You take time and money to wrap a gift and then give it to a person. He/she takes it and tears the wrapping paper and throws that wrapping paper in the waste paper basket and then somebody has to take it and put in the garbage can. Then the garbage man takes it by garbage truck to the dump and throws it in a pile, which has to be bulldozed to compact it and make it part of the earth.

In India for a serial to be shown on TV, approximately 30% of the show time has to be sold to advertisers at a predetermined rate/min. We all know that in US to advertise on Super Bowl football game each 30 seconds advertisement is sold in millions of dollars. The shows, which cannot bring the expected revenue for the network, are canceled. Some shows in the US that have been on, for more than 40 years, are still popular with viewers.

Bartering : Earlier, you bartered potatoes for onions if you had plenty for yourselves. You always give what you have more of, to get what you have less of. This really very profound statement and is true for everybody and applies to everything without exception.

Prostitution was the first business in the world where you exchanged money for services.

If you keep things, which you have not used for three years, then you should give them to somebody who can use. The three year cycle is used because, like winter clothes you have may not be used if you have mild winter for a year or two so you need to keep at least for three years and in no case more than five years. There is talk of recession and people have been laid off by larger companies and many of the small companies with sales less than $250,000 and medium sized companies having sales of $10 million and less have gone out of business. This has caused people to look at what they barely need to survive. People in U.S. have the tendency to live luxuriously. That is why they bought houses, which they really could not afford and buy all the goods, made in China, because they are cheap and not because they had to have them. If all of us go through the things in our houses, we could see that we can live comfortably with only 10-20% of the things we have in your house.

When we were growing up in India, I vividly remember that we used to collect old newspapers and sell them. We also used to sell our old clothes, people used to go to houses to exchange old clothes with pots and pans. Since most of the Indians living in US now will not have much problem going back to conserving energy and material things. Many of us are used to low cost of energy, we do not plan well when driving a car to find the best route to go several places that we want to go to. We all leave the lights on in the rooms we are not using. Now since the cost of energy has gone up because the World is using more energy, we all have to conserve energy. India and China are using 50% more energy in a year than the previous year. I recently visited Dubai and the construction projects going on are phenomenal. They are developing many buildings with thousands of houses. They have also built the tallest building in the world with 160 stories. They have constructed a locality called 'The Palm' where they have filled the ocean almost 390 feet to build this development.

This has been a smart move on the part of the ruler of Dubai, who knows that his revenue from oil will be almost over by 2015 and hence he has built Dubai into a heaven of sorts making it a tourist attraction and business center for the world, like Switzerland used to be at one time. Now all the countries have asked for accession to Swiss bank accounts by most of the countries so that they can track the illegal money hidden by individuals or corporations of the country.

One of the most important numbers to judge the wealth of the country is to see its GDP (Gross Domestic Product). The country, which has the highest per capita income, has the best economy. Dividing the GDP with the population derives the per capita income. These numbers are shown for few countries as follows to make my point:

Country	GDP	Per Capita Income	Population In millions
United States	14,364,163	37,500	320
China	7,916,429	4990	1,300
Japan	4,354,368	28,600	160
India	3,288,345	2800	1,200

Table I

Only five years ago, United States, Japan, and United Kingdom were the leaders.

Now what has happened is that India and China have been growing approximately 8-10 per cent per year and the other countries are in the 2-4 percent range.

This phenomenon can be explained as follows:

Dr. D. K. Rangnekar (who happened to be my brother-in-law and who started Economic Times of India) wrote in 1966 a four-part editorial in his paper. It blamed the Congress Government for asking all the foreign companies operating in India at that time to get out of the country, or if they wanted to stay in India they could own only 49% of the company and the Indian partner would have 51% of the investment. Who in the right mind would want to invest money in India at a time, when the economy was very bad and the GDP might have been one tenth of today and so would be the per capita income. In 1991, Mr. Manmohan Singh became the finance minister and asked foreign companies to come to India and not under strict conditions. The difference was that Mr. Manmohan Singh like Dr. Rangnekar is an economist. Dr. Rangnekar was a leading economist in India and was given Padma Shree Award posthumously and was also selected as one of the two individuals honored by 'Time' Magazine in 1974 to be a world leader and what he did would change the world in the 1975-2000 spans.

It is good example that politicians like those in the Nehru family ruined the country, while smart economists can run the country much better. I can say the same thing about US politics in 2012 being run by politicians.

Mr. Singh realized that India did not have the technical expertise at that time to produce and market products economically. Most factories at that time were very old and had manual mode of production of goods because India had a lot of people. But, now the world knows that the Indian people are very smart and they have proved that by reaching various parts of the world and doing well.

Another interesting statistics is that approximately 2 million Indians in USA have almost two times per capita income in USA as compared to the average income. Presently India graduates 1,000,000 students from colleges per year.

You must have seen that in 2007, President George Bush went to India for the first time and try to tell Manmohan Singh that we are two democratic countries and together represent 310 + 1200 = 1510 million people and we should work together. The week before Mr. Bush came to India, he had visited China and wanted to talk about the balance of payments between USA and China and had said that it was very lopsided. Manmohan Singh knew that, so he told Bush, "Well, you will have to change the balance of payment between India and USA, which is only $28 billion and with it is China $279 billion, then we will talk about working closely together.

In an earlier chapter, it was mentioned that Shri (Mr. in Indian language) Lokmanya Tilak decided to fight the British with knowledge and not with weapons, to gain independence.

China went ahead of most of the countries because a forward thinking person (as mentioned in the book written by Friedman—World is Flat) took a Chinese town of 50,000 people and taught them English and set up assembly lines for manufacturing products with cheap Chinese labor and went all over the World to promote building in China with cheap labor and not much restrictions. We all know what has happened now that most of the goods we buy all over the world, even in India is made in China. Another instance in particular was the uniforms the United States Olympic teams wore to the open ceremonies of the 2012 Olympics. The dresses were designed by American designer, Ralph Lauren but were completely made in China—due to the price differential.

If an economist instead of a politician had run India in 1966 instead of 1991, (twenty five year difference) what good could not have happened to the Indian economy? We all know that a pool of good technical expertise was available in India. India also had wood, oil, coal, gas and iron and most of the other things required to manufacture goods. You can see over the time, from 1966 countries like Japan, Taiwan, Korea, Philippines, Thailand, Indonesia, Vietnam and Cambodia prospered. All these countries do not have the essential resources to manufacture goods. When I was working in Seattle, I used to see used American built cars, burned to get rid of the plastic and compressed for shipment to Japan and other countries, to build new cars from that steel and ship them to USA to eventually take over the American market. Even used wood products were shipped to Japan and they built TV cabinets and other things and sent them to USA to later take over the USA market.

Back in 1975, when I came back from a visit to India, I went to a Sears Department store and my kids wanted cashews to eat. When in India they had asked to buy cashews, but they were not readily available and what was available was almost $10 per pound. I was surprised to see the price in the Sears store was $2 per pound, so I asked the server, where the cashews came from. He told me that they came from India. It puzzled me and I wanted to know why cashews were very expensive in India. I found that most of the cashews, other nuts and fruits are sold before the crop is harvested. Thinking that there will be a good crop they were sold at a low price. Other reason was that in those days, India wanted foreign exchange (US dollars). The cashew crop that year was not good and only a small quantity was available to sell in India and hence the price went up that high.

Another instance was when I was going through a mall in Tampa, Florida when I had just arrived in 1977. It was very cold in the mall during the summer month. So I asked the Dean of the College of Engineering at University of South Florida, why they waste energy by cooling to low temperature (around 70 degrees F). He told me that it is saving energy by keeping at 70oF, because to remove the humidity from the air they have to cool the air to 55oC and then they have heat it up to 70oC. If they had to keep it at higher than 70oC they will use more energy.

People, in economy, always worry about what they have lost and what they ought to have done to avoid those losses. You incurred those losses because you did not have information to predict it. This may be true in any economic transaction you make to buy or sell assets. I always tell myself that "What is lost belongs to somebody and not you and you should now think about protecting what you have left".

The standard of living in India is low, but the cost of living is very high. If one wants to live in India with the same standard of living in USA, it costs at least 50% more in dollars than in US. The mere fact is that the manmade goods are expensive in US, while machine made goods are less expensive. If you look at your budget for the family you find that approximately 80% is spent on machine made things and only 20% is spent on manmade goods. In US, since machine made are cheap, your cost of living is lower than in India (some bits on economy of scales, revenue generation through taxation and expense by the government on a larger population adds to costs). Average income in 2008 in India was $1,200 per year while in US it was $14,000 per year. If you wanted to buy Honda Accord it cost $ 18,000 while in India the same car cost Rs.18, 00,000 (which in 2012 exchange rate of Rs.55 for 1 dollar) was equivalent to $32,800 so, if one bought Honda Accord in India he/she had to work for 35 years without spending money to buy anything else. While in US he/she has to work only 1.28 years to do the same thing.

And so it happened for baby boom,—the soldiers came from war to there wives and created that boom. This has put quite a strain on our economy and of social security administration.

SCIENCE AND TECHNOLOGY:

It is said that it is good to sleep under a tree because it is beneficial for the tree. When you breathe you take in oxygen and breath out carbon dioxide, which trees use to make chlorophyll.

When we go in the forest, we get cockle burrs on your clothes. Someone to develop what we call Velcro used this knowledge. It is used on shoes to bring two surfaces together and also in caps and in many other ways.

To keep the brain active, you need 6-8 hours of sleep. The people who take daytime naps outperform non-nappers on memory exercises. And, surprisingly, a mere 6 minutes of shut-eye is enough to refresh the mind. Falling asleep in nap triggers a brain-boosting neurobiological process that remains effective regardless of how long you snooze.

Being deprived of sleep even for one night makes the brain unstable and prone to sudden shutdowns akin to a power failure—brief lapses that hover between sleep and wakefulness, researchers say. "It's as though the brain is both asleep and awake and they are switching between each other very rapidly," said Prof. David Dinges of the University of Pennsylvania School Of Medicine, whose study was published in the Journal of Neuroscience.

"Imagine you are sitting in a room watching a movie with the lights on. In a stable brain, the lights stay on all the time. In a sleepy brain, the lights suddenly go off."

The findings suggest that people who are sleep-deprived alternate between periods of near-normal brain function and dramatic lapses in attention and visual processing. This involves more structures changing than we have ever seen before, but changing just during theses lapses.

He and his colleagues did brain imaging studies on 24 adults who performed simple tasks involving visual attention when they were well rested and when they had missed a night's sleep.

Dr. Joe Pachorek states that he is constantly surprised at how many of his patients he sees who have trouble sleeping at night. Trouble falling asleep, waking several times a night, or just staying asleep are common problems effecting millions of Americans across the country. He wonders about how many people could remember when they went to sleep the right away, slept straight through the night and woke up refreshed in the morning. He bets that it would have been a long time since most people could say they had a truly deep, restful night of sleep. Sleep problems seem to be an unfortunate fact

63

of modern adult living—but why is that and what can be done about it? Most Americans either resign themselves to the thought that there is nothing they can do, so they just suffer or go to a doctor who often simply writes a prescription for sleeping pills.

Following tips help you keep your brain active:

> **Flex it**—You have got to use your brain to make it stronger with fun and memory strengthening exercises.

> **Feed it**—The foliate-rich goods may protect your brain just like a bike helmet.

> **Socialize it**—Here is why staying in touch with friends and family is important, so that you get more neurons.

The best way to go to sleep quickly is to read something you are interested in, think about all good thoughts and also do meditation.

There is Newton's Law, that every action has equal and opposite reaction. If you do anything good in your life you get paid by good things in your life. If you do anything bad you get equally bad things happening to you in your life. During your life span you start with a score of zero and end with the score of zero. There are so many instances in the world of this. When you commit a crime the laws puts you in jail or you get life sentence or death. That is why I always preach that do not lie, steal or do anything bad in life, since you will have to pay for your sins in your present life. The one keeping the score is no other than your own brain. Hindu philosophy says that you have many lives and you may not pay for in this life.

You do not have to eat to find out what can happen by taking poison. We use the information in the literature and do not challenge it. If there is some other issue like that which does not involve possibility of death you challenge it and do it.

I compare the human body to a car. You know when the tires on the car get worn out, you do not throw the car away, but install new tires, and it is true of battery, brakes, windshield wipers, paint, and engine parts. It is true with human body; you replace knees, hips, and eyes, use hearing aid. I am on the Faculty Advisory Board of University of Florida. It has good Medical and Engineering Departments and have education program for Bio-medical Engineering careers

This is one of the biggest reasons I support Bio-medical Engineering, because I want them to design replacement of all the human organs. I always talk to kids in college to take bio-medical engineering so that they can make better human parts for replacement so that we can live longer. We all remember that before the artificial heart was fine tuned, it used to be such a large equipment that they could not put in your body. But, now they are replacing human heart very successfully and you do not hear about that many deaths with heart attack. I have said before that heart has been working hard for us. My heart has been beating for 3,819,000,000 times. It is calculated by multiplying heart beat/min by 1440 minutes per daytime; multiply with 365 days per year, multiplied with number of years you have been living. If you take an elastic on your undergarments, they lose their resilience when they are washed for may be maximum of 250 times. This is called hysterisis, for loosing elasticity over a time period. So you have to respect your heart for it is doing for you and take good care of it by having better and stress free life.

Dying with natural causes We all know that an automobile dies of natural causes, which are similar to the ones, that human being die of, because of normal wear and tear on each moving part in the automobiles and human beings. I have had both knees replaced, like you replace tires on automobile. I may need my heart replaced like you replace battery in the automobile. It is true of lights, horn, and paint, seats replaced in automobile and eyes, ears, face for human beings.

You flex your knees many times during the lifetime of a person. If one is careful during the lifetime one can extend the life of the knee flexing quite significantly. One must use better shoes to walk, walk carefully and do not hustle if you have time to get there. It is also true that if you use the brakes on the car by driving fast and then stopping suddenly using brakes. This makes the life of the tire shorter. Also we know that you take the curves while driving fast then you cut down the life of the tires. And you can see how you can increase the life of your knees. Now, since so many new medications are available that by using **Glucosamine** you can extend the life of your original knees.

You should do breathing exercises while you are driving or you are waiting to see someone, or whenever you have a spare moment.

To keep salt from absorbing moisture and coagulating, it is good to put some rice grains in the saltshaker. The rice absorbs the water and keeps salt from agglomerating.

Friction is loss of energy. Lesser the friction, lesser is the energy used. Since there is such a shortage of energy nowadays, we need to design anything with as low friction as possible. We all know that when you get older, the knees start aching. The cause is that the cartilage, which is the lubricant, has been destroyed and hence when you move the knee, the friction between the knee joints aches.

In Europe, for many years now, when electric motors or other moving parts are designed, they put special emphasis on reducing friction between moving parts and hence all the electrical motors in Europe have an excellent usage rating. We all know in US we are the biggest user of energy and since until now we had plenty of energy available, we never designed for less friction but we designed for looks and convenience. It is also noted that now a days a lot of plastic parts are used to reduce friction. In US we waste a lot of energy.

When you cook rice and want each individual grain to be separate, what you do is coat each grain with butter so their surfaces are not is hydrophilic. This has do be done with complete mixing of butter and rice. When the rice is boiling and even before you stir it so that each grain gets coated with butter, because the butter is melted and coats the rice grains uniformly.

As mentioned before, even checking one grain of rice, whether it is cooked or not, is sufficient to determine whether all the grains are cooked. In this case you are using only one sample for the entire rice grain population, which must be in thousands of grains.

When we make *puri* (which is part of the Indian bread family) it puffs up. The *puri* is made with flour and it contains a lot of starch. You have to roll the dough and make it evenly thick then put that in a vessel with hot oil, the bottom of the *puri* gets cooked and since it is starch based it make an impervious layer. Then you normally dip the *puri* with a spatula or put hot oil on top of it. The *puri* gets cooked and makes impervious layer on top, too. Now that both sides are impervious, the water and air trapped inside expands and make *puri* puff. I used to make coated paper, where you coat paper with starch and then send it to the dryer so that the starch cooks and make an impervious surface, but sometimes it used to make blisters similar to what happens when you are making *puri*.

When you have pain in the muscles, you use hot water bag or a heating pad. The reason you do that, you want to heat the blood, which is flowing in the body to be thin. You also use drugs like Plavix to thin the blood. The word thin and thick are ambiguous words, they really do not clearly define the condition of the blood, for that matter of any liquid. In Chemical Engineering there is a term called Reynolds Number (again 'number' is important).

The Reynolds number is defined as follows:

$$\text{REYNOLDS NUMBER} = \frac{D * V * d}{M}$$

D = Diameter of the pipe (vein in case of human being)
V = Velocity of the fluid in the pipe (blood in case of Human being)
D = density of the fluid (density of the blood in case of Human being)
M = Viscosity of the fluid (viscosity of blood in case of Human being)

The most important part of this equation is the viscosity of the liquid. When you heat a liquid, then the viscosity of liquid goes down and hence the Reynolds number increases, that means the liquid can flow much easily. Normally, if the Reynolds number is less than 2300, it is called laminar flow, the liquid is flowing slowly and the blood going from and to the heart at this number is more lethargic and slow. This can cause problem of blood circulation and chance of a heart attack. If the Reynolds number is higher, then the blood is in turbulent flow and the blood moves nicely in the veins and arteries and chance of heart attack is not there.

Now if you consider the other part of this Reynolds Number. In the numerator is the number for diameter of the pipe, vein. When this diameter goes down because of plugging, then the Reynolds number goes down and you have lower Reynolds number and again you have the potential risk of a heart attack. In humans, we call this as cholesterol building in the veins and it reduces the diameter of the vein and hence lowers the Reynolds Number. We again use medication to reduce the cholesterol and/or you adopt a proper diet with low cholesterol.

The following drawing shows how restrictions that reduce the diameter of the pipe create a tremendous amount of pressure loss and hence you have to use more pressure to deliver the same amount of fluid as, when there was no restriction. This situation is similar to the cholesterol build-up in the veins, and hence you have to have higher blood pressure from the heart to deliver the amount of blood that is needed to satisfy the oxygen demand for the brain and other parts of the body.

I work with manufacture of Calcium carbonate and when it starts building up in the process pipes I use a Roto-rooter that is what exactly a heart surgeon does with angioplasty, when arteries have cholesterol buildup.

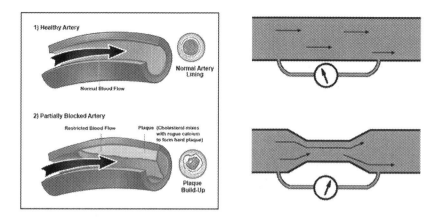

Figure 2: ARTERIES AND VEINS—SHOW
CHOLESTROL BUILDUP

I drew a similarity between the human body and an automobile. Human beings are like a car in the sense that you replace the parts and make it basically like new. Like my father used to do, getting old cars from England and while teaching students, rebuilding them like new.

I got my knees replaced, and I call that rethreading the tires. If I need a new heart, it is like replacing the battery in the car. The heart is a human pump and arteries are like pipes or tubes in the car. If I need a hearing aid, it is like fixing the horn on the car. If I need new liver, it is like an oil filter in the car. The nose also filters the air; it is like air filter in the car. If I need new kidneys, it is also like a filter in the car. We eat food and breathe in air (21% oxygen); it is like fuel and air mixture to run the car. This analogy can go on and on.

Actually the human body is like a big chemical factory where all kinds of unit operations go on like filtering, pumping and so on.

This is the main reason I recommend students to go in Bio-medical Engineering. These students can develop body parts to replace the malfunctioning body parts. I have a goal to live 104 years since my great grandfather lived for 103 years. My great grandfather had a factory to build horse carriages for ***Maharajas*** in India since they wanted traditional style and not the 'modern' automobiles.

Numbers are useful to know what to do further. In India, today the middle class, with disposable income, is 400 million strong. Based on this data, TATA has built base model car, costing Rs. 100,000 (if you take Rs.50 per dollar) it comes to $2000. It is also known that India has 700 million cell phones. This is because you do not have go through the trouble of getting a landline, which may take a long time. In the 50's in India to own a telephone was a luxury and see what has happened now. Even people who do not have sufficient income have a cell phone. I found this is so because you can get a service wherein if you receive calls, you do not have to pay for them. So the vendors use it for customers to call them and they rarely call out.

When my granddaughter was one year old, I used to take her to the back yard of their house. In October, when the leaves turn in color and then fall, I told her why it happens. The chlorophyll in the leaves disappears because of the weather, the minerals which are in the leaf show their color because of its metal component. She did remember it, when she got older.

It is know in Chemical Engineering that the rate of any heat and mass transfer is given by the following equation:

$Q = U*A*$(temperature difference).
Q = rate of mass or heat transfer
U = Coefficient this is determined by quantitative analysis of the system being studied
A = Transfer area, in square meters, or square inches.

(Temperature difference) = Difference of the temperature of the hot body you transfer from to the temperature of the cold body you are transferring to.

Greater the A (area exposed for the transfer), faster is the rate of transfer. U is defined as the transfer coefficient and is determined by actually doing experiments. The higher the temperature difference, greater is the transfer rate. The best example of this is drying of clothes. If you take a towel and crumble it and let it dry, then the drying time is higher, than when the towel is spread out. The reason is the area exposed for drying when crumbled is much less than when it is spread out. This is the reason we hang clothes on strings so that more area is exposed (front and back of the clothes) and it can dry sooner. You can use wind also to dry faster because in that case the dry hot air can take the moisture away from the wet body.

The pressure is defined as pound force per unit area. For sharp pencil point, lb/sq is very high since the area, which has that force, is very small, and hence can poke the skin, but when you will use the other end of pencil with the eraser will not poke and make a hole in the skin since the area to exert the same pressure is larger.

As sugar crystals in many other countries are larger, it takes more time to dissolve, as compared to, in US, because in US the sugar is in a more powdered form and has smaller particles. The smaller particles for the same weight have more surface area and hence can dissolve fast.

While cooking, the professional cooks always cut onions used for cooking very small so that they can cook more uniformly and fast because more area is exposed. Since most of the onions get the heat uniformly. If the onion pieces are large then the inside of the pieces do not get heat as much as the outside, hence outside burns and inside does not cook.

When you buy shoes, which are made of full leather, they are not able to distribute the weight of the body since it does not absorb the pressure. But, if you use tennis shoes, which have air cushions, the total weight of the body is absorbed by the air cushions and your feet do not hurt. You have seen in the last 10-15 years most of the people have started wearing tennis shoes, which were previously used only to play games.

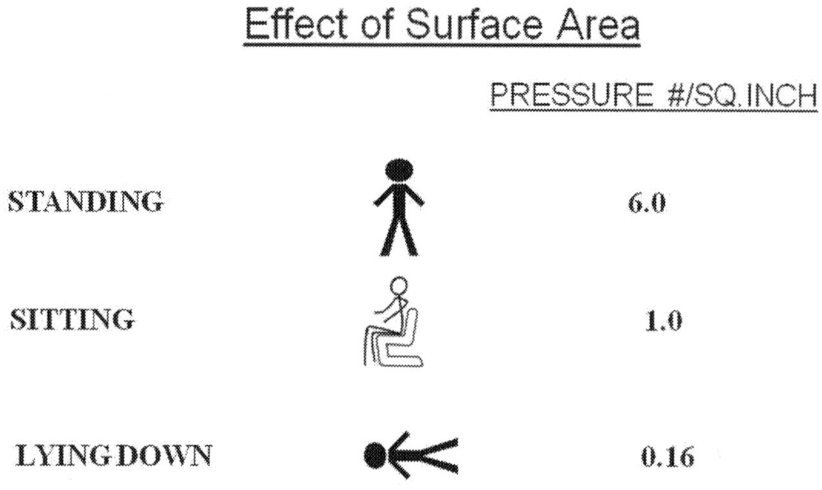

Effect of Surface Area

PRESSURE #/SQ.INCH

STANDING		6.0
SITTING		1.0
LYING DOWN		0.16

Figure 3: Effect of Surface Area

One more point is that I have the following rule: If you can sit do not stand, if you can lie down do not sit. This is based on the pressure difference. Pressure, as defined earlier is weight per unit area.

1. When you are standing the whole body weight (say 180 pounds) is taken by the two feet, which there are is say 30 square inches, so the pressure on the feet is 180 divided by 30, which is 6 pounds/square inches.
2. When you are sitting down you have larger area—your feet plus you two thighs, which will be 30 sq. in plus 150 sq. inches for the thighs, a total of 180 square inches and hence the pressure is 180 divide by 180, which is only 1.0 pounds per sq. inches.
3. When you are lying down, then the total area will be 1120 square inches, so the pressure will be only 180 divided by 1120, which is only 0.16 pounds per square inches.

So you can see go from 6.0 pounds/sq. in to 1.0 pound/ sq. in to only 0.16 pounds/sq. in

When we are holding on anything to support ourselves, if you hold it lightly it will fall, but if you hold firmly then it will not fall. This is because you are holding lightly; the area of contact you are using is much less than when you are holding firmly.

So you can see even in our normal daily life you should have the maximum surface area for anything you do.

PERSONAL AND OTHER IMPORTANT INFORMATION:

My daughter, when she was 30 months old, swallowed a small compass (I still have that in my possession) and we over reacted and scared her and made her feel that swallowing is a big problem. We were in India at that time and then in Bombay there were only two X-Ray machines and it being lunchtime they were closed. When we finally got the X-ray we could see clearly the compass in her stomach. When she was growing up she got a lot of allergies and she had to take medication for it. When she was about seven years old, she had an acute asthma attack and had to take her to the hospital. On our way to the hospital because my daughter could not breathe she asked me, "Dad, am I going to die?" As soon as we reached the hospital they put her in an oxygen tent. When we came home from the hospital, we found that the pills she was supposed to be taking, she was throwing them behind the couch. What had happened in her swallowing incident in India made her scared of swallowing and was throwing those pills away.

When we used to go in the elevator we used to stomp in the elevator and at that time did not realize that she would later not go in the elevator till this day. Of course when herself forces her she sometimes now does go on the elevator. This also made her not to fly and enter any space where she could not see an exit. Hence she was not willing to fly. When her children were able to fly, she became strong and started flying because she wanted her kids to explore other countries.

Each person has some goals in life and mine has always been to visit all countries in the world to know more about how people live, which would become part of my statistics, thereby, increasing my database to make informed decisions. Since I have been traveling I appreciate that USA is the best country to live and raise my family. I have visited India more than 50 times since I have been here since 1956, there is still lot of dirt and filth and corruption and I could not live there. There are billions of people in the world who do not have good food to eat and shelter to live in.

As a family, we have taken many trips together and my oldest granddaughter has been to 31 countries—going around the World two times. I was very proud of my daughter that she started flying without any problems. Till now, I myself have been to 88 countries and I wanted to visit all of them. Approximately 30 years ago there were only 96 countries in the world, but now with the division of countries like Russia, Yugoslavia and others there are 192 countries in the world and it will keep on increasing because most of the countries want to be divided on ethnic, religious, language basis.

When the children were in elementary school, we used to take them away from school for as much as 8 weeks; it did not bother their ranking in the school. They were getting a lot of exposure to the world, which was a lot of information. My wife also made sure that they did their schoolwork when they were away from school.

My cousin had come to see me in US and he is always interested in refurbished old cars. I was taking him to a beach, where I normally take my visitors; on the way he saw lots of vintage cars. I have gone that way more than 100 times and I never saw even one of those places. I am not interested in vintage cars. The same was true about him, when I was taking him to my daughter's house; he saw an old house, which had vintage car. I have been that way more than 100 times and never saw that. When we visited the person who had that car, he took us behind his house and where he had a workshop to refurbish cars. That is his hobby.

For any party or marriage and other such functions, the person who is ready to send the invitation for such occasions has to set up a list as priority. How do you make this list? You have say 200 potential invitees, you make a list starting with the closest people first by giving those first numerical numbers, and then you go to your second priority and third priority till you have invited the number of invitees you wish to invite. So we always put number for each individual. The number of invitees is made first by checking the expenses what you are willing to incur. So when that number is reached you discard all the others who did not make the list.

While counting the number of invited people, you need to assume that normally approximately 15% of the final number you have of invitees, will not show up, so you should always plan for 85% of the number of people who say they will attend 2-3 days before the function will come. This is particularly true of the food you order for the party.

When you have any function where you need to make sitting arrangements, you again use priorities to determine who sits where. This again goes by how they rank in your personal numerical ranking system. In the later part of this book, I mention the four circles of life, in the first circle are your closest relatives, your parents, your wife/husband, your kids, your son-in-laws, your daughters-in-law and your grandkids, the second circle are your brothers, sisters, their families, your closest friends, third circle is your acquaintances, and the fourth circle is everybody else. You are in the circle based on your statistical number as to how many times you talk to them, talk about them, and see them per unit time (days, months . . .).

Nowadays when you go to wedding functions, the tables are not numbered so that you cannot tell where you are seating how the person who has invited you respects you. Low number means you are close and larger numbers mean you are not well regarded by the invitee. And now instead using numbers to designate the table, they use names of cities or countries or any other names that the wedding party likes. You still can tell how the priority is based on where is your table is set up in view of the main table.

If you are going to, say buy a car, you start looking at the cars at the dealers but every car on the road you see, you are collecting information, so when you are ready to buy you can use that information as statistics to make a good decision. It is true of any item you are intending to buy—you watch out for them, when you see those items.

If you are deciding what kind of roof you want to put on your house that you are building, you look at every roof of the housing you see. If you were not trying to make that decision of the type of roof, you may not look at even one roof.

You always hear that people who need people are the luckiest people in the world. For me, the loneliness is the worst disease in the world. I hate to stay at my house by myself and also hate the most when I go to restaurant by myself.

You need to know how to deal with bad habit so you can be a better person. One of my granddaughters gets really upset when she loses in any competitive games and I try to rub it in on her. To combat this, my daughter uses a technique, which I think is very good. What she does is she goes to another place and count up to ten. The trick is to ask her to count backward from ten to one. This makes one more conscious than counting from one to ten because counting like normal does not make you think and you do not loose the thought that you have lost.

When I come through the Paris airport, I see many people complaining about the attitudes of the French people. The travelers feel that they get least attention from the airport personnel. On May 11, 2009 Air France flight no. AF218 was delayed and the airline personnel again ill-treated Indian passengers. The airline then apologized for the ill treatment and said that it understood the annoyance expressed by some of them. Exceptional circumstances made the situation particularly difficult.

There are only three countries that have half hour time differential between them and Greenwich time, rest of the countries have full hour time differential. So to call some countries it is difficult to determine the time at the country. Since there are so many people living away from their homeland, they call quite often. To call at the right time is dependent on the time at the country you are calling from to the country you are calling. The 24-hour cycle time has to be manipulated to find the right time to call. For instance to call India from US, it also depends on the time in U S which is either 9 ½ or 10½ so it is easier to subtract 2½ hours or 1½ hours and make am to pm or pm to am. In India, they use half an hour time differential from Greenwich time so that they did not want to have two time zones in India.

You need to give attention to *end of life* issues. We all know we are not eternal and the life expectancy in US in 2010 for men is 77 and for women it is 81. So when people are approaching that age, the family needs to decide how to take care of them at that time. Due to the affluence, assisted living places are doing great business. Few years' back this was not an option for younger family to take care of their kids and at the time take care of aging parents.

How do we fulfill our childhood dreams? When I used to go to Elephantine College in Bombay, India, there was a watch shop near the entrance of the college and I used to see Rolex watches there. So I said to myself, the first time I can afford a Rolex watch, I will buy it. While coming to USA in 1956, to go to college, I stopped to sightsee in France and Switzerland and I bought myself a Rolex watch.

Decisions that you make are based on your surroundings and the information, which you store in your brain. I still have that watch, but I now use a newer watch. Really the newer Rolex is very heavy and does not have the features of digital watches that come at a fraction of the price. It was true about the cars, I bought. When I was growing up in India, my father had Automobile engineering school since 1922, he used to get MG, Rolls Royce cars from England and teach kids to repair them and then we would use it for few months and then my father would sell them. At that time also, for safety, Mercedes Benz was the best car on the market. Cadillac was supposed to be the most luxurious car. So when I could afford a Mercedes Benz, I bought one. I bought Mercedes for 25 years and then I started buying Cadillac.

I am from India and having been in US since 1956, presently I am working in India; Indian business people are having problems paying me as a US person since they know I am an Indian. India had been under the British rule for such a long time that Indians feel that Caucasian people working in India are smarter than natives. One of my relatives told me that you are fair enough and your mannerism is American, but your name is wrong. You should change your name from VASANT CHAPNERKAR to VINCENT CHAPMAN. Only then they will pay your travel expenses by Business Class and pay your consulting fees that they would pay an American. We, in India, have what I call is, a White Skin Syndrome. Whenever I have taken White Americans to work with me, they pay their business class airfare ticket and pay them their consulting fees and that is the only time they pay my business class airfare ticket. Talking with some others from other underdeveloped or developing countries, I observed that it is true for them also. When people who have come to live in US, go back to their native country, they say also, witness the White Skin Syndrome. They will pay White skin people to do a work, but will not pay their own people who have migrated to USA and want to work in their native country.

One of the many real life experiences, about which I have mentioned in the earlier paragraph, goes as follows: In 1971, I was traveling with my young son to India on an Air India plane. It was a Boeing 747, which had three coach class compartments. At that time, I could not afford to go by either First Class or Business Class. I had been to the New York airport about seven hours before my flight's departure to India. At that time, you could not make your seat reservations ahead of time. So I was given the boarding pass and as I was going from the first compartment to the third compartment, where my seat was assigned, I saw mostly white people in the first compartment, there were mostly white and Indians without kids in the second compartment and in the third compartment there were only Indians mostly with kids. When the owner of Air India, J. R. D. Tata had come to receive the *Tony Janus Award* in Tampa in 1978, my wife and I were invited to attend the function. You might know that the first commercial flight in US was from St. Petersburg to Tampa flown by Tony Janus.

At the end of the function, I went to Mr. Tata and told him about my experience about treating Indians on the Air India flight to Bombay. The following month I got a formal letter from Air India saying that the company would not repeat what had happened and that Indians should patronize Air India. I have since then never gone to India on Air India flight and have been to India 56 times since then.

Why am I the only one in my family that is well educated? When my mother died in 1944, I was asked for, by my mother to be with her before she died in the hospital. I was only twelve years old then. I always think that she wanted to bless me and till today I always think that she is watching out for me. Actually she is ever in my thoughts. I believe that she has helped me get through my life and succeed at whatever I tried to accomplish.

When I had cataract surgery, I asked my Doctor to make one eye short sighted and the other long-sighted. This way I do not need to corrective glasses all the time and still could read and see long distance with my two eyes.

When traveling, I always break the journey into at least three parts, so when I reach the second part of my journey, I think that I have accomplished one third of my journey and feel good about it. I then go on with my second and third parts till I reach my final destination.

When my grandkids were growing up we took several long trips (around the World, Southeast Asia, India, Western Europe, England, Ireland, Scotland, and South America, South Africa) we always talked about what we could do in the future. My oldest granddaughter used to say that kids like coke and Chocolate, and she said why don't we make bottle of Chocolate and fill it with Coke. When she recently graduated from high school and went college, I told her, 'you know that the CEO of Pepsi Cola is an Indian Woman'? You should strive to be CEO of Coca Cola.

Why do we send flowers and cards? To me this is to satisfy your heart and has nothing to do with satisfying your statistics. You can use the same money for better causes. This is quite essential for the people who think from the heart and not from the brain. Only, that I remember, I bought flowers in 1967, for my wife when she was coming from India, but she missed her flight and did not come for two more days and the flowers wilted. Since then I have never bought flowers. Sending cards—what really happens that you go to the store buy a card and pay for it. Then you take it home and write the address and put a stamp on it and leave in your mailbox. The postman then takes to the post office and puts their stamp on it and delivers the next day or some time later to the same mailbox where he had picked that up. The person brings that card in the house and then opens and read it and after a few days throws in the waste paper basket. In order avoid the money and time spent in doing so, I have a solution. I take my wife to the store where I buy the cards from and let her read it and keep it back on the shelf. This way I have avoided all that money and time we spend on this card to send it. I know it sounds very cruel and heartless, but it is the truth. You always need to think from your brain and not from your heart, since heart does not have information to be logical and works out of passion, and we know it is not good.

I have always carried an India One Rupee note in my wallet. The reason is that the note has written on it all the fourteen major languages spoken in India. The script of all the languages is different. Printed on the note is 'One Rupee' written in 14 languages, since we then had only 14 states, then. You can see that India is not only one country but made up of many major factions. The food they eat, clothes they wear, and the how they look is quite different. Most of the Indians I have specifically talked about it do not even know that these languages are printed on the India currency notes. They represented the states in India some time back, now there are many more states, the same way as Russia and Yugoslavia and other countries have. You know why India is not really one country but 28 now, each having its own language, culture and food. It is like Europe—France, Germany, Switzerland, and Belgium.

When you are listening to a lecture, it is wiser to keep your eyes shut so that you can hear every word without distraction. I know when I am listening with my eyes open my eyes wander and cannot concentrate on hearing.

Why do we feel guilty? If you have done something that you should not have done, then you feel guilty. You should always get rid of the guilt as soon as possible by taking corrective action. This will give closure to the issue and you will be free from that guilt, which is very essential to get on with your life.

In the book, 'I am OK, You are OK', the author tries to make you think positively while accepting that we both are OK, but, what I got out of the book is that everyone has a child inside them at any age. The people who have lived long think that it is not good to let the child in you come out, so they act with reservations and that creates the conflict in your thinking and you do not try to remember when you were a child. By letting your childlike feelings come out at any age, it does not create the conflict and you can live a very satisfying life style. I, at 80 years, still let my child inside come out and play with my grandkids as if I am their age. It is do things, which are fun for you. For me it is to play with grandkids, travel, and read. For each hour you spend in these activities, you get two hours of extra life. Now I am closer to be 81, I ask people that when I show them number 81, I ask them what they from their side. They always say that it looks like 18, so I tell them I have a heart transfer a heart from 18 year old. I always get a laugh. As I said before that laughing is the best medicine.

The other book, which has had a tremendous effect on me, is the book written by Norman Vincent Peale, 'The art of positive thinking'. You can always look at a half glass as either half full or half empty. The positive thinkers think it as half full and negative thinkers think as half empty. I always think that when you have any problem think of it as not a problem but the opportunity to do a good.

One of the good books that have had an influence on me is the art of remembering. Memory is so important that you can be successful if you can retrieve from your brain whatever information you need at the instant you need. The people with quick thinking ability are called genius because they can retrieve any important information they need right away, and without causing any confusion in obtaining the desired information.

You have to keep in mind that you do not cram non-important statistical information in your brain, but develop the power to solve problems and look for relevant information you need to solve that problem. When I got my Master's degree, I learnt what I should have learnt in my Bachelor's degree program. What the Master's and Ph.D. degrees taught me is—how to solve problems and not just remember all the facts. For my Ph. D. program in Chemical Engineering we had open book exams. We could go to the library with the examination paper and use the information available in the library books and journals to solve the problems. It is again done so that you can get more detailed information you need from the library so that you solve the problem with your method of thinking. This does not mean that you should not have any statistical information in your brain.

I have a cousin in India who goes in businesses he is not familiar with or has any expertise. Whenever I talk to him about planning and making market study before starting a project, he always tells me that if I start thinking and planning then I will not do any other business and he continues not doing anything at all.

When traveling in different countries what gives you the best reception if you greet them and ask how they are? What is their name? The answer is use of their native language. It breaks the barrier of you being different from them. In such cases, we have found in our travels, you get what you want from the local people.

Because we have been in US since long and also have Christian son-in-law and daughter-in-law and we go to local churches, mosques and synagogues and of course temples, since we came from India. We have adopted what we call world religion and take good things from all religions. They really preach the same thing; treat all people, as you want them to treat you.

I can drive in any city or town in the world. I have found that the street signs and other signs are kept such a way that they are either hidden by the sign in front of it or they are on the wrong side of the road which one would not normally look.

When I am not sure and my driver in India is not sure either, the best way I take, to find a place, is to hire a local taxi to take you to that address. As I have said many times, that time is the most important commodity and you should save as much as possible. Earlier, often the driver used to say that he knew where we were going and would then wander off, wasting time and gasoline. So I decided to get the local taxi so that I can follow the taxi, because he belongs to that area and has better statistics (information) on how to get to my destination. It also helps my nerves when I am taken to the place where I am going in the least possible time and shortest route. In India, the Global Positioning System and good road maps are not available like in US and hence you have to depend on ways like mine. In the US there are excellent detailed maps and the GPS system is very readily available. Now most of the expensive cars (approximately $20,000 and up), have a GPS system built in the car. Also, handheld GPS system like Garvin is still available at a very reasonable price.

Sometimes you become overconfident, it is better to go to the ocean or lake and look at the water. When you do that it makes you realize that you are not as big as you think because you are infinitesimal as compared to the body of water. I also go to the ocean or lake when I am feeling low and that makes me feel good to look at that mass of water, which has calming influence on me.

When I was in Australia and New Zealand, I saw a lot of sheep. There are 60 million sheep in Australia and only 20 million people. You always see the sheep with their head down and eating. In New Zealand there are 20 million sheep and only 3 million people. I think these countries are the best to visit for visitors like me because they have lot of facilities to visit. There is the Barrier Reef, Philippe Island and Ayers Rock.

When you are still charging an appliance or a computer, if it is fully charged, then you should not charge anymore, because it still keeps on using electricity and you waste that much electricity.

I do not think that there is any person who does not want to win in what he/she is pursuing. It is our instinct. The art is to try to win and if you do not win, give yourself credit for what you have done and not be dejected, but tell yourself that I will analyze why I lost and then have a new strategy to win. We should always keep a score on anything we do and make sure that is overall positive and if it is negative, you deal with it.

Remote controls are now being used to save time and energy. In earlier days, in the fifties, TVs did not have remote system. So when you changed the channel or volume, you had to get up and go the TV and change it manually. I think with the introduction of remotes for TV and stereo and video players, the term **Couch Potato** has been introduced. This is because you do not get any exercise and you eat and get fat. The statistics in US is that an average person watches 7 hours of TV. Of course, some do not watch at all, but people in hospitals, who do not like to move, watch TV almost all the time they are awake. It is better to restrict kids watching too much TV and not watch shows which can give them wrong influence in life.

DVR is the best invention for me. I always record all TV shows, except for sports, and watch those shows by fast-forwarding the commercials. For any TV show to be on the air, there must have one third of the time sold for commercials otherwise it is not successful. Hence by recording on DVR and watching later I can watch three shows in the time of two shows.

I am always looking for ways to reduce time or energy usage, since time is important and the cost of energy is going up exponentially. I went to the club to use Jacuzzi, and found that they heat the water in the Jacuzzi to 100oC. I noticed that it is being used quite sparingly. So I suggested to the management of the club to keep the water temperature to 90 or 80oC most of the time and when somebody comes to use Jacuzzi and signs in, you should have a remote with the desk clerk so that he can increase the temperature to 100oC, since by the time the person goes to the Men's or Women's room to change the clothes and take shower, the water in the Jacuzzi will reach 100oC and as soon the person leaves you can decrease again by the remote.

When you are brushing your teeth in the morning you run the tap of water and use it only may be 10-20% of the time. The best way is to open and close and another way to reduce is to turn the water valve under the sink half closed. It is wise to turn the valve on that line under the sink partially closed to reduce significantly the use of water.

My wife was very active in places where we lived, because she was extrovert and started social and cultural clubs for the Indians and she would always be the head. In places where we lived she was called Indira Gandhi (the woman Prime Minister of India). Of course, she would always talk. When she used to be master of ceremonies for cultural and social clubs and always used to say that my husband opens his mouth, only when he has to yawn. Since I started my consulting company in 1984, I have started to talk a lot to sell myself to my clients to sell my paper technology all over the world. My son now jokes, 'Dad you talk to the dog also and you still keep on talking when that dog has left you'.

Whenever you do any task you should not give up when you get no answer or you cannot sell your idea. You always need to try at least two times before you give up. We have the tendency to quit after the first try. Trying more times than one and keep trying till you succeed is called 'persistence'.

People say that you have to make a lot of money so that you can sleep better, but in India the people work and sleep on the streets, sleep extremely well. So I guess it is not good to make a lot of money if it is going to take away your biggest asset of sleeping well at night. The person who can sleep 6 hours at night is the well-balanced person, since he performs his chores without any time for tension or depression. If you cannot sleep at night then you have problems doing things during the day. You if you have a lot of money you can do what you want but then cannot sleep, because either you have made that money illegally or by cheating other people. You know what has happened all over the world in 2009 and that many of these ruthless people ought to be in jail and I am sure they have hard time sleeping. In US, most of the prescriptions written by doctors are sleeping pills, Valium and anti-depressants. So make all the money you can make in a way that it does not deprive you of your biggest asset, which is a good night sleep. The good sleep can range from 4-10 hrs depending on the person.

Why we individually like some things more than others?

We know that certain people like certain things. Some of us have not even tasted some foods and we do not like them. When you have eaten something and you got some improvement in your being, then you like that. It is also true that if you tried something and you did not like it for any reason you stay away from it. I realized, that I like sour and sweet things to eat. Also I like vegetables, which are juicy like eggplant; okra . . . there is a fish in India called Bombay duck, which is slimy and hence I like it. I have not been able to pinpoint why I like those things. I am sure there is an incidence in my life, which prompted to do that way. Feel, smell, taste are individual choices we make, and it has to be based on your life style. If you have to drink lot of milk when you were young, to the point that you start hating it, because you were forced to have it, you do not like it when you grow up and then there is no authority to tell you that you have to. All this depends on the statistical information stored in your brain. According to Hindu philosophy you have many births and deaths and you may like or not like something now because you encountered something which you either liked or did not like in your earlier lives.

When you are feeling good, everything looks okay to you. If not, then even small thing bothers you. You should have a closure as soon as possible on the things that bother you, or else you wasting good energy.

You should do things because you want to. If you are forced and you do not want to do it, it is usually a disaster.

So never blame anybody, if you take his or her advice and have a disaster. You have to take responsibility of what you do.

Every action performed by every individual is performed with a specific purpose in mind. Some do good deeds and some perform bad ones. No one can remain inactive for even a moment and no action is performed without a purpose. It may appear strange, but it is true. You may think that there are evil people who harm others for no reason. Also there are saints who help others for no reason. In reality, there is a reason even behind these actions.

An evil person finds pleasure in harming others. So to experience happiness he causes harm. Similarly, a Saint gets happiness in seeing the welfare of others. Thus a Saint serves others to get happiness for himself. And for all of us as well, the motive behind achieving wealth, health, wife, son, fame and beauty is one—*happiness*. This proves that without any teaching or training every individual wants happiness and nobody wants sorrow, grief or pain. Happiness, bliss and peace are all synonyms for God.

Since I came from India, women at the time I was growing did not go to work and stayed home and did cooking, raising kids. I still think it is a good system. Like I have written before, in our family, women stay home for at least first four years of the child's life. Since women have been demanding equality with men, the world has changed. This has also changed economy. Women can work now and make good money and hence are not dependent on their husband's money. It has been changing in India and now women are very independent because they can make the money for themselves.

Since the time I have been in the US, I have seen those parents tell the kids when they are 18 years old they have to have their own money for 'extras' and even for college education and hence there are summer jobs. Summer is supposed to be holidays for kids and they should not be working. In India, and Indian parents here, normally pay for college and do not demand that the children work in summer. I think personally working in summer is not a bad idea, since it teaches the 'value of money'. I encouraged my kids to work in summer and Christmas holidays so that they can appreciate the fact that to make money you have to work hard. I did this mostly because when they were going to school, the kids asked me for more spending on the weekends and they appreciated my giving money.

PERORATION

The foregoing would perhaps reinforce the raison d'etre of the entire book—why is information important? It is said that the large the island of knowledge, the longer the shoreline of wonder. Similarly, it is only when we actively and consciously collect data to help us make right decisions, we realize, how little we know and how much there is to know. It is an important exercise because in India, for example, if you end up in a wrong hospital, you might end up even loosing your life and you might save it if you have the information about where you can be treated well. So information is important, because the decisions pertain to you, your family, and your life. No outsider will bring it on a platter and offer it to you, even if you are ready to pay for it. You have to collect and use your own information systematically and wisely.

৪৩

Chapter 4

Relationships

A person isn't who they are during the last conversation you had with them—they're who they've been throughout your whole relationship.

Rainer Maria Rilke

Cᴽ

Prime / Premiere . . .

Epicurus said, "You don't develop courage by being happy in your relationships everyday. You develop it by surviving difficult times and challenging adversity".

All conflicts in the world are created first between people or groups of people. Each one of us is supposed to theoretically get along with everybody else. This, I call *Utopia*. Since every one of us is brought up with different statistical information given to us by our parents, teachers, and our friends and since all of us are selfish and think that our way of thinking is the right way, we cannot get along. Can you think, why a young man crashes a 767 jet into a building, knowing very well that he is going to die and is going to kill everybody in that plane?

In life we have relationships with others. Each one has different relationships with others based on his/her statistics.

There are three circles:

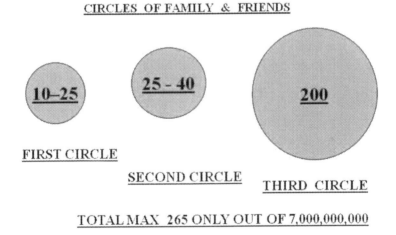

Figure 4: Circles of Relationships

CIRCLES OF FAMILY

The first circle has your closest relatives—father, mother, husband, wife, children, son-in-laws, daughter-in-laws and grandchildren.

The second circle has your brothers, sisters, cousins, other relatives and very close friends.

The third circle is your close acquaintances and friends.

THE 4TH CIRCLE:

Includes all other people in the world, which is a population of about 7,000,000,000.

The person's being in a circle depends on the statistical fact, as to how many times in a unit time period, you think about them, talk to them and see them.

Based on this, the first circle for an individual will have 10 to 25 people. The second circle may have 20 to 40 people. The third circle may have 200 people. The people in the fourth circle are there because they do not have anything to do with you. If they did want to come in the second or third circle they will talk to you and invite you.

I usually try to contact persons in the fourth circle two times and if I do not get good response I forget about them and do not waste my energy by talking about them negatively.

Those outside the third circle are people based on the statistical information you have and based on that you do not want to associate with them or they do not want to associate with you.

The criteria for being in the circle include the interaction between the individual and the other person.

If you add the people in the first three circles are only 230 to 265 people. You know in the world there are more than 7,000,000,000 people and it should be easy for anybody to select the people in your three circles.

All of us know that we waste more energy by dealing with people who are not in your circle and hence should be avoided. This will leave you more energy to give it to the people in your three circles.

The criteria for being in the circle are the interaction between the individual and the other person. Presently my individual statistics on the relationship is the wife I live with and my children and especially my grandchildren. I have been blessed with my family who also wants to interact with me on a daily basis. We talk to each other on the phone on a daily basis.

Nowadays, since the communication is good and quite cheap we can do this. When I came to the U.S. in 1956, calling India was very expensive as compared to your income, and hence, I did call India for the first five years very rarely till 1990s. Now I can talk anywhere in the world any time and it is very inexpensive. In the fifties, to communicate with India, I used to write a letter and it reached India after two to three weeks and then I got the reply after another two to three weeks. Now another big communication mode is e-mail and it is the best way of communication since you do not have to think about time of the day, which is very critical for phone calls because of the time difference around the World.

Based on the communication now, I use not only my statistical information, but I have the access to use the statistical information of my children and even my grandchildren. Hence, now I know that for me to make a wrong decision is very rare. My wife and I were the only decision makers when my children were less than 10 years old. In a way it was good in only respect when we wanted to go to any restaurant or movies, the decision was very easy for me. When my kids started giving their opinions based on their statistical information it was very difficult to agree, since each one had their favorite restaurant based on their likes and dislikes. Till this day my children keep on telling me that you want us to think for ourselves and we are doing that now. It is interesting to note that if anything bad happens either dad or grandpa did it and if it is good, they take the credit for it.

This brings to the point of discussing why each child was different, though they were from the same household. The reason for this the environment to bring up the child is different based on the conditions existing at that time. Usually the first born child gets all the attention and does not have to fight for anything, but, when the second, third or more children are involved the environment is different; the parent's life is a lot different at different times based on their statistics at the time. Usually the second, third and more children have to compete for everything. It is always that the first born that gets what he / she wants up to a point that the money is available. Initially you are making just enough to make both ends meet. In later life you are making more money and you can buy better things for your second or third child. Till this day my oldest daughter always says that she had to drive older cars and the second one had better cars and the third one got brand new cars to drive.

We do not realize that every person is selfish and so any relationship is based on how the environment is at that time. Most of us say that I am not selfish. I think that everyone is selfish and chooses the alternatives in any conflict or situation, which suits him, the most. I always say that if you hold a piece of bread in your hand and that is the only thing available to eat and there are ten children who need it and if one of those kids is yours, whom will you give that piece of bread?—Of course, your own child.

Human beings are involved in an intense "struggle for existence," competing for limited resources. This idea helped Darwin uncover the mechanisms he needed.

Combining the idea of competition with his other observations, Darwin explained how evolution could have occurred. First, he stated that ***variation exists among individuals of a species***. Second, he stated that ***scarcity of resources in burgeoning population would lead to competition between individuals of the same species because all use the same limited resources***. Such competition would lead to the death of some individuals, while others would survive. From this reasoning Darwin concluded that ***individuals having advantageous*** *variations are more likely to survive and reproduce than those without the advantageous variations.*

The normal relationship between husband and wife is very important for the family to prosper. This does not mean you cannot have different opinions, but you have to make sure that relationship is good.

In the United States, the divorce rate is 54.8%, while when I was growing up in India up to the late fifties; the divorce rate was 0.5%. I am sure, as India gets more affluent; the women will not be subservient to men and will ask for divorce. Most of the divorces in India when I was growing up were in show business, now days called **Bollywood.** Now since the women are more independent the divorce rate in India is going up and is presently estimated to be 1.1% of married population. Prosperity in India has increased the divorce rate. This is the price you pay for having higher economic standard.

Divorce is to me the worst type of relationship for the family, which is unfortunately involved. Divorce affects all individuals of the family. Personally for me to have close relationship with a person, it is important to get along with the person. How I can have a close relationship with one whom I cannot get along with. And to think that he/she took vows to stay together for the rest of the life. Now the younger generation is apt to disagree with the mate and get divorce. In my generations and earlier, the marriage was everlasting. I have been married since 1958 and though we have many differences I never think that divorce is the solution, because I know that it is not. My children have been married since 1983, 1993 and 1994. In U S statistics is that most of the kids who are in trouble are from divorced parents. They have seen unpleasant arguments, beating in the house while they were growing up and think that it is all right for them to do. Again it is what the statistical information that they get in the house.

The troubled kids of divorce parents get involved with drugs, crime and some of them end up in jail. The U S Government spends more money on criminals than it costs to send a kid to school and college.

The normal relationship between the wife and the mother of the person is usually strained. The main reason for this is that the mother says that I have had my son, gave him birth and raised him till now and now how you can say he is yours. Again based on the statistical information, which the mother has about having and raising her son is so large and vivid that she is not able to forget. By the same token the wife says that I have been with the son for some time and raising a family with him and he will be with me the rest of his life and hope to be much longer than he was with the mother.

The same is true of the relationship between the sister and sister-in-law. The sister says that he is been with me since they were born. Sister has been with the brother since they grew up together and stayed together till he was married to the sister-in-law. Again they have a lot of memories with each other and that is their statistical information. The sister-in-law says like the wife in the above paragraph, that now he is mine and he is going to live with me the rest of his life and have a happy family with him.

The relationship in the above paragraph can be illustrated very vividly by the following episode. Once I was visiting a friend of ours who had been to India for the wedding of her brother. She was proudly showing a big album containing might be hundred pictures. When I was going through the album I saw only one picture in there, which was upside down. As soon as I saw that picture upside down, I confidently said that it must be your sister-in-law and sure enough she was. This again proves to me the power of statistical information gives you the expected outcome. She kept on saying, no I love my sister-in-law. Then why was her picture only upside down. This shows again that the brain has no other information than the statistical information. When people talk about conscience and sub-conscience, there is just one information and that is the truth.

If all relationships are based on honesty then there is no problem. Hypocrisy always gets you in trouble, because then you are not truthful.

What happens when there are differences between people? Both the sides want to win the argument, both start arguing a lot and no one wants to give up? In such cases I say, if we solve it amicably then for me it is 2+2= 6 but, if you argue and do not come to conclusion then I say, it is 2-2=-2. The addition total comes to 6 because it has synergistic effect. When you argue the total outcome is—2 because both parties loose. You know that if you win an argument and the other person looses, he is going to try to get even with you and make you lose the next argument. Mahatma Gandhi says that if someone slaps you on one cheek you offer him the other cheek to slap.

As I mentioned before about relationship with kids, whatever bad things happen to the family it is always the fault of the father. For this reason I have formed a Battered Fathers Association and nobody wants to join me. I think they still want to keep good relationship with their kids because they will need them in their later life.

In relationship with wives, I have also a club called Battered Husbands Association. I have no members. I asked my daughter's father-in-law to join; he quickly said that I would have to ask my wife if I could join. As soon as he said that I knew he is scared of his wife and will not join.

As said earlier, how you raise kids is very important. If you are affluent and want to reward kids for good behavior you can give them new cars and any other expensive items and if they have been properly raised they will not abuse that privilege. So I call them GOOD SPOILED KIDS. These are the kids who still have good values. In our family we have bought new expensive cars and none of the kids have misused that privilege. I call kids who use these privileges and do not exhibit good values, and drive fast and show-off as BAD SPOILED KIDS.

When I was working in North Carolina in the early sixties, I went to work after getting my Ph.D. in Chemical Engineering. I had not experienced life in a small city in the US. The town I worked was a small town in the mountains of North Carolina. Being a city boy from Bombay, India, I did not know how people in small town in US live. One of the employees was making fun of me all the time. When I asked him why you are doing this to me, he said that when you like somebody you tease him or her. So I told him I do not like it. He did not talk to me for few days. After few days, I told him you can kid me but not like me so much you have to kid all the time, and I will appreciate if do not like me so much, since I missed being teased by him. Another fellow employee was making fun of me that I came from a big city like, Bombay (population now almost 21 million). I was talking to him about having a flower and vegetable garden in my back yard. So I was watering weeds, thinking they were flowering plants (Zinnia) and the neighbors told me that they were ragweeds. So this employee brought me rag weeds in small paper cups and told me they were Zinnia plants and wanted me to take them home and plant them. Since I knew the difference between Zinnia and ragweeds I told him why are you trying to fool me, I know they are ragweeds and not Zinnia plants.

The town in North Carolina, where we lived was Brevard. In the 1984 issue of Money Magazine, it was voted as the Number 1 city to live in USA.

Raising the kids in this small city (population of only 6500) was very good, especially in the late sixties and early seventies, when hippy movement was going on.

Everybody should provide for his or her later life and not be dependent on anybody else, even your own children. Even if your children will take care of you later in life, it is good for our ego to be independent and live by themselves as long as possible. Many families (I really do not know what percentage) do not take care of their parents because they say that they need their money to take care their own family, means wife and children.

When we are not able to stay on our own, we normally go to either Assisted Living Facilities or stay with your most compatible child. When you do that if you take a room, which was occupied by the children, then there is a lot of conflict. Every one of our children, when they built their latest houses, where they are staying now, have a dedicated bedroom for my wife and me. This way you have separation and you do not come in each other's way to have any scope for conflict.

If you are a football fan, you know that the receiver has to have separation from the defensive guy to complete a pass, if not then the pass is not completed.

All of us think that we have relationship with God and do everything with his blessing and also always tell the truth. But, consider why sometimes telling a lie is okay. For instance, consider the following story and decide whether telling a lie is all right in this case:

A priest was watering his plants in the front of his house. The priest saw a cow came running and went in particular direction. Then, a butcher followed the cow, and he asked the priest in which direction the cow went. In this case if he tells the truth to the butcher, he will go and kill the cow, but, if you lie and send him in another direction, then he will not be able to kill the cow.

Another similar situation arose when Nathuram Godse killed Mahatma Gandhi in January 1948. Godse thought that Mahatma Gandhi was giving his country to run by Muslim leader, and Godse being Hindu did not like it, so he killed him to save his country from being run by Muslim Leader. His action was wrong to kill Gandhi, but his motive was right. I am sure Godse knew that if he killed Gandhi, he will be caught and will have death penalty, which is what happened. I admire his guts, to give up his life for the sake of his country. He did not have any other mode to get done what he wanted to do, by going to court.

My wife had a friend in India, whom she had known before coming to USA. In the nineties when my wife and I used go to India every 2-3 years, then, we used to stay with her. She used to run her own business and she was a very proud lady. Once when we were talking I told her that as per your desire, I sent a $150 cheque to a school in Miami. She vehemently said that you did not send it. Now, how she could make such a statement, had she seen all the cheques I had written to make that kind of profound statement and also imply that I was lying. What people say is sometimes very derogatory without any proof to back it. Of course I did not see her after that and sent her a letter to return the money she had borrowed from me. She never contacted me again and I forgot it as a bad experience in life and closed that chapter.

When you are talking about what gives you the most sorrow. It has been listed that the following priority takes place:

1. Loss of mate
2. Loss of job and so on

When you are talking to any agent you buy goods or services from, they always ask so many personal questions about you, such as name, address, and phone numbers. When they do that to me then, I always say how come you do not give me your address and phone number, as a joke. I also always say, when they ask what I can do for you. Actually they are asking that question with reference to what the previous conversation was. But, then I say that send me a million dollars, and then say that I will be good guy and in good mood and will let you keep the first million dollars and send me the next million dollars. I always get a laugh.

When our family was growing up in USA, we used to go to India every three years, to see our relatives. Since we were married in US and the kids were born here, we always had to decide how to spend the short time in India most beneficially. We found that each of us knew our own relatives much more than the others, we decided it was wise for me to stay mostly with my relatives and for my wife to stay most of the time with her relatives, so that we can reminisce our childhood with the people whom we grew up with India. This way we did not have any conflicts.

If you see the relationship between husband and wife, we know that the women live longer than men. You have never heard that you need to find a rich widower, you always find rich widows.

And you almost always see bald men and not bald women, because women dominate the men. I come from old tradition from India and my wife does not dominate, still I am going bald. This means I think I am dominating, but actually I am not. In Assisted Living Facilities you find almost 3 women for one man.

We always have a debate about men and women. The brains of men and women are different. Women play three sets for tennis matches, while men play five sets. The placing of Tee in Golf is further back for men than for women. The taxi drivers in the military are mostly men. Women are likely to be more sentimental and have more emotions and passions than men. For men passion is usually a goal they want to reach. If somebody tells me that he/she is speaking from the heart, I do not listen to him or her, because heart is just a pump and has no information to make any kind of decision. Heart does not have statistics stored to be used to make the decision. This is why you see more emotion in women. You rarely see a man crying, unless it is a very bad situation, but women cry very easily.

Women often experience depression after a baby is born. Women have puzzled over it for years—why the heck do men do the things they do? Why do they profess their love for you one minute, then ignore you the next. Why can they not remember our birthdays? Let science explain some of these conundrums and help you improve your relationships.

The hippocampus, where initial memories are formed, occupies a smaller percent of the men's brain than the female brain. If on your first date he cannot remember where you work, even though you told him all about it when you met, just remember that size matters, hippocampus size, that is. Do not take it personally.

Do not expect the man to get the hints. If you have a crush on him, you may have to put it out there, because men are not as skilled as women at reading subtle emotional cues. As Dr. Larry Cahill of the University of California at Irvine puts it, "we have been assuming that the ways in which emotions are organized in the brain are essentially similar in men and women," but they are not. Parts of the limbic cortex, which is involved in emotional responses, are smaller in men than in women. Additionally, scientists at McMaster University have found that guys have a smaller density of neurons in areas of the temporal lobe that deal with language processing.

That's why it is probably a good idea to tell him straight up how you are feeling. Expecting him to infer from your hints could leave both of you scratching your heads. Guys in general just are not as verbally adept as women. Large parts of the cortex—the brain's outer layer that does a big art of recognizing and using subtle language cues—are thinner in men than they are in women.

In fact, since I have been writing this book for over twenty years, I discuss my point of view on my paper technology and life with the people I meet, to get their input.

Does man seem to be "up" most of the time? It's not your imagination: Male brains produce 52% more serotonin (the chemical that influences mood) than female brains, according to the study done at McGill University. The studies show that fewer men than women suffer from depression. I am always in high spirits when I get up in the morning and till I go to bed at night. I feel this is because, statistically I can expect what is going to happen and my mind is prepared for whatever happens. In case my wife, if she has not seen somebody for more than twenty years, she still feels that she is attached to them and want to meet them and be friends like they were before. I keep on telling her, if they cared for you they will want to call you and enquire about you if you have made contact with them and they have not responded. This is clearly shown in my figures on 'Relationships'.

In males, the pre-optic area of the hypothalamus is greater in volume, in cross-sectional area and in the number of cells. In men, this area is more than two times larger than in women, and it contains twice as many cells. This area of the hypothalamus is in charge of mating behavior. This is responsible for the release of sex hormones. Men are more intimate all the time than women, because of the brain-based differences.

Exploring the neurobiology of politics, scientists have found that liberals manage ambiguity and conflict better than conservatives because of how their brains work. Scientists at New York University and the University of California at Los Angeles showed through a simple experiment in the journal of Nature Neuroscience that political orientation is related to differences in how the brain process information.

Sulloway says that liberals were 4.9 times more likely than conservatives to show activity in the brain circuits that deal with conflicts and were 2.2 times more likely to score in the top half of the distribution for accuracy.

For the first time in history, through recent breakthroughs in neuroscience, experts are able to observe brain activity while we are in the act of feeling—and their findings have been astonishing. Once believed to be lumps of lonely gray matter cogitating between our ears, our brains turn out to be more like interloped, WiFi octopi with invisible tentacles slithering in all directions, at every moment, constantly picking up messages we are not aware of and prompting reactions-including illnesses—in ways never before understood.

Brain scanning has showed that a key region called the dorsal striatum, a dopamine-rich pleasure center, became active when they tested the milkshake, but not when they tested the comparison liquid that just mimicked saliva. The brain was less active in overweight people than in lean people.

The Richest man in the world, Mr. Buffett's brain is influenced by the statistics driven approach of Ben Graham, his Columbia University business professor. When picking winners out of the herd it helps to have his caliber acumen. He insists that involves little more than common sense, the kind that comes from educating yourself broadly across multiple disciplines. "Learn your gaps", and fill them. He recommends you get three textbooks on the subject and skim them, "it's a good start". That is what he does.

When you make friendships, other than your close relatives, it is always best to choose friends for long-term relationship who are economically, socially and educationally of similar status. I have seen relationships with not having the above, and then the stronger one takes advantage of the weaker person.

When you are raising kids, there are many good things that parents can do. Most Americans have seen TV on Bob Hope Show in the eighties, a three-year-old Tiger Woods playing golf. I had a similar experience when we were raising our son. I used to take him to kindergarten in Suite and a tie. This made him dress well in his life. When after graduation he was looking for a job, he said that I have to work with Xerox, because they have the best training for marketing people. In Xerox training course he was told that you have to wear the best tie to make good impression. Hence, when I was working in Italy, I had to buy for him, hand painted silk ties from Florence, Italy where fashions are born. So he always told me that you created this monster dresser and now you have deal with it.

When the kids are 2-3 years old, their brains seem to send multiple messages to the body at once—eat, scream, spill juice, throw crayons—and good luck to anyone trying to form complete sentences or thought in their presence. The density of neural connections in the 2-year-old prefrontal cortex is far higher than in adults, and the levels of neurotransmitters, the mind's chemical messengers, are lower.

Now a days the parents always ask the question—Are kids too busy? Rushing from school to soccer practice to piano lessons to science club meetings is no new thing for many parents. The studies, based on data about how children spend their days, show that only a minority is heavily scheduled and that organized activities are linked to positive outcomes in school, emotional development, family life and behavior. The children most at risk have no activities at all.

When you have good kids, it is equivalent to a lot of money in the bank. In fact you cannot put a price on that. Hence I have emphasized in this book that raising kids the right way is the most important thing parents can do. Our kids and grandkids have traveled all over the world. When we used to take them out of school (unto 10th grade) to tour the world, they did their studies and the teachers always said that having the experience of traveling is extremely good for them to be good students and citizens.

Segregation:

As mentioned in my Preface, when I came to USA in 1956, I was going from Pennsylvania to Gainesville Florida to study for my Ph.D. degree in Chemical Engineering; I stopped in Washington DC at the bus terminal. I wanted to go to restroom and when I came to the restroom I saw two rooms for Men, one was marked White and other was marked Black. I was surprised and I looked at the color of my skin, and saw that it was not white or black, since I thought it was closer to white than black I went to the restroom marked white.

In 1957, when I was studying in Chemical Engineering at University of Florida, I went by car to Tallahassee to meet a girl who had traveled on the ship with my classmate from University of Bombay and now was studying at University of Florida. When we reached Tallahassee we went to AW Drive-in and asked for food, the waiter told us that she couldn't serve us since we were not white.

My wife, who happened to be from India, had come to do her Ph.D. in political science at Florida State University. Since she was very good in giving lectures on India and women in India, the President of the Florida A & M University in Tallahassee invited her. When the President came to pick her up at the Graduate House on Copeland Street, my wife asked him to come in and that she can get ready to go with him. He told her that if I come in you would not be allowed to stay in the Graduate House, so he better wait for her outside.

Gainesville was equally racially discriminating. An intelligent real estate person built a housing development in 1959 and sold all the houses to white family, except for one house, which he kept for himself. What he did was when the development was completely sold out; he brought a black family to stay in the house he had kept for himself. As soon the others saw this, all of them unloaded their house at lower prices to get out of the neighbor hood. He then made the black family to leave and sold those houses again. I do not know how many times he must have done this.

When my wife and I got married, I decided that I had enough of studying and decided to drive to Chicago where my cousin was living to look for a job. On the way my wife had a headache, we stopped at a drug store in Ashburn, Georgia. When we sat at the table, the waitress came and told us that we do not serve non-citizens of USA. What she really meant was we serve only white people. We told her that we were students and will be citizens when we graduate. That did not make any difference and she would not serve us drinks so that my wife could not take her medicine and we had to go to the counter and get the drink. It appears at that time the segregation and integration was going through a big revolution and the blacks in USA were demanding equality.

Once, when my wife was invited to talk, the University of Florida had started integrating and had a black student in Law School. When my wife was on that panel, the Law student told the audience that when he went to the restaurant (probably the same one we went to in Ashburn, Georgia) he was told by the waitress that we do not feed Negros, so he replied that I do not eat Negros, I eat hamburgers.

We all know what happened in Alabama and all over the South in the following years, and eventually President Lyndon Johnson passed laws against segregation. We have come a long way since then. This was quite evident in 2008, when US elected Obama as President. To me, President Obama is really not black, since his mother was a white woman from Kansas. Even so when the African American population in US is only 12%, he got more than 90% of the votes from African American to win the election. So quite a few, white people voted for him.

White men almost never marry a Negro girl, they do not mind marrying Asian or Hispanic girls. There are many instances that Asian or Hispanic girls married a Negro, but it is almost always very well educated Negro man. So to me. in any relationship you need to have same interests and it is usually similar economic, social cultural level.

In India there is similar kind of segregation (like blacks in the USA) and is based on the caste system. It is based on the family, the community you are born in.

1. Is called **Brahmin**. It is postulated that the Brahmins came from the head of the God and are supposed to be learned and had studied the '**Bhagwat Geeta**' and they are the one who perform all ceremonies for God. They are supposed to be the smart people. They were supposed to be white in skin color.
2. Is called **Kshatriya** and they came from the body of God. These are the warriors and rulers who are strong and take care of the mankind. They are not much educated. They were supposed to be red in skin color.
3. Is **Vaisyas** and came from the hands of the God. They include craftsmen who use their hands to do their work. They are Carpenters, Blacksmiths, Goldsmiths, men who make sculptures. They are also not well educated. They were supposed to be brown in skin color.
4. Is called **Sudras**. They are supposed to have come from the feet of God and do all menial jobs like those of janitor, hairdresser, and cobblers. They have practically no education at all. They are not allowed to go to the Hindu temples. They are supposed to be black in skin color.

The good part of this segregation in India is that if they dressed alike, you cannot tell one from the other. In practice you can tell by the clothes they were because of their low-income level.

In my case I come from the blacksmith family. Luckily for me, my immediate family was quite rich because they were business people. Our skin color was white and similar to Brahmin's color. But these color definitions are not exact and hence they could not be differentiated if they wore same clothes. We wore much better clothes than anybody else in 1940-1970. Afterwards the caste system was nonexistent because most of the people from all castes started getting good education and started earning better. In school and college in India, when I used to go with my Brahmin friends everybody thought that I was Brahmin and they were lower caste since I was white (by Indian standards) and wore good clothes.

PERORATION

Franklin D. Roosevelt said, "If civilization is to survive, we must cultivate the science of human relationships—the ability of all peoples, of all kinds, to live together, in the same world at peace."

ℰℐ

Bibliography

http://www.brainyquote.com/quotes/keywords/statistics. html#Fd93ErVQoxwX7tS0.99

Chapter 5

Normality

We need international support so that our people live a life of normality, of dignity, of liberty and freedom. I hope that our cry for freedom may be heard.

Mahmoud Abbas

ᘓ

Prime / Premiere . . .

It is said that a good liar should have a great memory—to remember the different lies he has told to different people

What is normal? Every person has a norm for every activity and is dependent on his statistical information. This normality is fluid because it changes all the time depending on the newer statistical information that is collected every instant.

Always telling the truth and not stealing should be everybody's norm. When you tell lies then you cannot keep track of what you told to whom. Living an honest life without cheating or stealing is always the best. Nixon is a good example of this. When he had the Watergate problem, if he would have come out and told the truth everybody would have forgiven him and he would not have to be impeached. Same is true for Clinton in his case.

You expect that the keyboard on typewriters should be the same all over the World. I travel a lot internationally, having more than 4 million miles on Delta. I go through Paris a lot and have also worked in France. It is quite interesting to know that the typewriters in France have different keyboards, the letters a, s, @ are in different locations compared to other typewriters all over the World. This is one kind of shift from normality.

Why are people investing in the growth of China and India (mostly) because the number, which they like, is the growth of GNP? In India and China for the last more than five years it is 8-10%. In the US and many developed countries it is only 3-5%. In 2006 in the investment in India was about 29 billion dollars, while in China it was 279 billion dollars.

Now-a-days in India, they also have shows like Indian Idol, Dancing with the Stars and the sets for these shows are as good as they are in U S, and may be better and more lavish. If the same shows were produced seven years ago it would not be lavish. I go to India quite often and I have noticed by counting to get my statistics, that in Mumbai, ten years ago less than 5% of the cars on the road were air conditioned, but today that number is almost 90% for private cars and about 10% of the taxis and local transport. In India two giant corporations have combined to buy new air-conditioned cars for the taxi drivers and take their old dilapidated cars (most of them are more than ten years old). These old taxis and old passenger cars normally wind up in smaller towns.

Due to the prosperity in India, women's status has changed drastically. Since old times in India, a day is celebrated called **Karvachowth.** On that the ladies pray to god to give them the same husband in next life. In earlier days in India, man was the bread earner and women stayed and look after the house and the kids. The man was supreme and women during those times did not speak or come and sit with visitors unless the husband asked her to. Even in earlier times if the husband died then the wife used to cremate herself in the fire of the husband's funeral. This is still practiced in very few places but law now abolishes it.

Black in the USA compare with the *untouchables* in India.

Why India has lagged behind China in their industrial development. If you are traveling on highways in China through rural areas, they have smartly put three hedges on the highway, the first hedge is approximately 3 ft high, and the second is about 6 ft high and third are big trees more than 8 ft high, but if you see in between the gaps of these hedges you see very badly kept houses and roads. The streets and roads in the cities and highways are always well kept by people constantly working on the sides of the roads. China very smartly designed city of Shanghai. They first built a big tower in the middle of the main city, and then from there on, they took a ten square block and demolished the old buildings and built modern buildings. The buzz in India is that Indians want to make Mumbai like Shanghai, but I think it has a long way to go.

Fiber optics first installed during the *dot com* boom, is now available for everybody to use all over the world. Though the *dot com* boom went bust, the fiber optics network had already been installed. With the false value of many companies like Red X, the money spent on fiber optics cannot be recovered by taking it out, but because of this the communications have improved tremendously and have become very cheap, about 10% from what it was before the fiber optics network was installed.

In order to avoid spoiling of food, you have to do two things, one is to keep it as cool as you can and second is to keep it away from air (oxygen in the air). The higher the temperature, the more is the rate of spoiling and higher the contact with air (oxygen in the air) the higher is the rate of spoiling. There are chemical reactions of the organics in the food with oxygen in the air. With every 10oC raise in the temperate the rate of spoiling doubles. This called the Arrhenius equation. When the conditions are not good then the bacteria grow and cause mildew

When I was at the dentist's I saw a chart of 'periodontal depth', which measures the recession of your gums, and again it is in numbers, which quantifies the condition.

We have been talking about thinking with the brain and not with the heart as statistically, you make the best decisions. Even while you are writing, your brain is still taking your hand to write, the hand cannot write without the command coming from the brain. We all know that there are many parts of the brain, which control different things in life. We know that when you have dementia, then your brain, which controlled the short-term memory, is dying. After that stage comes Alzheimer, when you lose long-term memory also.

It is customary in India to consider the birth date as the first Birthday and hence they always say the age of the person as that year running. In US the age is considered as the number of years you have lived and so really it is an anniversary of the birthday.

Normally there are many store signs or mall signs which are not readable in the time you pass by. They are cursive and also not good color contrasted. It is best to have yellow on black background or black on yellow background. International research has proved this to be the most noticeable color combination. That's why taxis are painted yellow and black

PERORATION

Vicente del Bosque said, "(Unfortunately) we are in a world that is quite extremist and extremism makes more noise. Normality does not sell.(And we are paying a high price for the existing abnormality)"

ॐ

Chapter 6

Trifles and Trivialities

I know that campaigns can seem small, and even silly. Trivial things become big distractions. Serious issues become sound bites. And the truth gets buried under an avalanche of money and advertising. If you're sick of hearing me approve this message, believe me—so am I.

Barack Obama.

ભ

Prime / Premiere . . .

"The thought that we're in competition with Russians or with Chinese is all a mistake, and trivial. We are one species, with a world to win".
George Wald

In this chapter we will discuss the normal words we use to express our opinion that are to me meaningless.

We use words like short, tall, big, small, high, and low. The reason we use these words is because not all people can estimate the exact measurements of what we are talking about, viz. weight in units (grams, pounds), height in units (inches, feet, yards, miles, cm . . .)

Words like luck, accident, old, hate, love, beautiful, ugly and retire have no meaning for me.

Rich and poor words do not mean anything. I am sure one who does not have means to have basic necessities is called poor, but rich can mean anything above that. To define rich, we have to know the worth of that person. We all know that the only way to decide that is how much money he has. Is a millionaire rich? Or one who has billions.

When people tell you that they do not have money to have a full life and talk about having good health. I do not know anybody will sell you anything unless you give him or her money, in return for what you get from him. Telling someone, I am a good person, does not mean that he is going to give you what you need, even something like food. You have to give him money.

I am always saying that three words in the English language I do not know what they mean are **Retire, Long** and **Old**. When you say the activity is long, you are already telling your body that it is going to be treacherous before you start that activity.

The word retire means to most people that you have done your service and now you are ready to take it easy and sit on your porch and see things go by. For one should never use that word because we have created that word to not much. Actually if you analyze that word **re** means again **tire** for the tire on the car. What we should say that I am tired of doing what I have been doing and now I want to do what I want, because I have attained financial strength to live the way I want till I die. We know everyone is going to die. I have heard people saying that I am retired and I am enjoying doing nothing. "Nothing" means no activity of any kind that means no eating, no breathing, and no thinking. That means you are dead. What people mean to say that now since I am retired I can do what I want, when I want? I am still working and do not plan to retire and do nothing, I am doing what I want and people still want my services with or without paying for it.

The word old means end of the line. A ten-year-old person can be old and a ninety-year person can be young. It is the way we look at the half full glass as half empty or half full. Our mental state determines your age. If you have good information through education, and travel, then you are always young and if do not have education and travel, then you think that you are old. You always have to want do some more than you have done the day before, if you do not want then you feel bad and feel old.

Bhagawat Gita states that we take birth with certain desires based on last life. If you have finished those desires, it may be when 10 years old or 90 years old you die. I still have a lot of desires and hence not willing to quit.

I have interesting story. Since I have started knitting, my daughter wanted me to knit a blanket for her. So I knitted her a blanket with baby blue and pink yarn. When my daughter looked at it she said "Dad" this for a newborn baby. So I said to her I would knit you another blanket with orange and blue yarns, which are colors of the Florida gators. Then remembering what I have learned from reading Gita, it will give me a few more years if I can live till I have first great grandchild to satisfy my new desire. Since my oldest grand-daughter is only 23 and she will not marry till she is 28 and then the first baby after 3 more years, I have from now 8 more years to satisfy my desire.

We always have to set some kind of standard, which has to be numerical to describe it.

When we talk about somebody being beautiful, it has been determined—that if the face of the person like, Cindy Crawford is looked at, they take her picture and determine the distances between eyes, ears, and nose, how similar they are on both sides of the center line. Then, like in contests of any kind the judges always give number between 1 and 10 describes the score. How do you think they give that score? It is only based on their own statistical information. To declare a winner you have many categories and there are many judges, which are picked from different backgrounds to make it more real. An independent company takes the numbers given by each judge and tabulates them by numbers and declares the one who has the most points as the winner. We have seen that 9.31 will win and 9.30 come in second.

In any sports you use numbers to keep the score and based on that score you declare the winner, in our daily lives, we also do it.

'Both are married', such comment does not automatically mean that they are married to each other. You have to say that they are married to each other.

We talk about calories we eat. We do not eat calories; we eat food, which is comprised of carbon, hydrogen, oxygen and many metallic ions. We eat the food and breathe air (with 21% oxygen) with our nose and ignite the food in the stomach to give us heat, which is measured in calories.

When you go to the doctor, the nurse always tell you he will take you in a minute, I always ask how many seconds are there in your minute. It is never 60 seconds but usually it is about 1000 seconds.

People, when they part from each other, say, that I will see you later? What does later mean?

When you are traveling, when you stop for directions to a place, the person always says go straight on this road, when he and you know that if you go straight you will land on the building in the front before a curve in the road. What he really means is that you follow the road. If you ask for what the distance is where you want to go, he always says it is around the corner; sometimes it has been miles around the corner.

This reminds me, when I was in Philippines, my host was taking me to the plant and while we were driving we were talking about our experiences in building roads in India and Philippines. In India, I told him that most of the roads are built very poorly and they need to be resurfaced more often than if they were built right the first time. My host told me that one contractor gets a contract to surface, say about ten miles, then he rebuilds the road and when he has come ten miles, he has to start rebuilding the road going back, because it has become ready to rebuild. So this contractor has a lifetime job of building this ten-mile track.

During any contests, when you hear first the praise, if it followed by the word "But" you know there is a problem and the contestant has not won. When you hear the word "If" you know there is something coming next is not pleasant.

If you are discussing something with anybody and when he says he has 3 or 4 houses, you know he is trying to avoid telling you how many. He has to know, if he owns it, that it is either 3 or 4 and there should be no question about it. If the numbers are large, then I can accept a wishy-washy answer.

We, many times use the word "best" very loosely. It may mean best in the world or restricted further by territory but we normally do not restrict by qualifying. That is why I do not like people telling me that they have the best TV, car, doctors, and of course their grandchildren (in the world). Because when they say—in the world, they actually know only a very scanty statistical sample. This may be that they know only ten doctors in one city and then say he is the best in the world. What everyone means to say that the best that they know.

Especially grandparents are the worst braggers of their grandkids. They always say my grandchild is the best looking, smartest and everything else. They know only few grandkids in the world and they make such comments, which is derogatory to people whom you are telling.

One grandfather was bragging about his grandchild and told me that their grandchild is only eight months old and he can recognize the song on the TV. I told him jokingly, to make a point, I said that my daughter is expecting a baby and was only four months pregnant and that baby also starts jumping in the stomach when that same song comes on TV.

I have friend, when I meet her she always says that my grandson is the best in the world. Then of course to tease her I also say that my grandson is best in the world. We all know there are millions of grandkids in the world and you may know may be no more than 50 other grandkids. Do you think that is a statistical sample, of course not? You can always say that my grandchild is the best for me and not involve the whole human population.

I have another friend, for him whatever he buys and uses, is the best. He never says it is not good, and even though sometimes I know he has made a bad decision, but he will still say it is the best. The best is being used so much that there is no qualification to it. If you stay in a town and you go to a doctor in your town and you may know may be five other doctors, you cannot say I have the best doctor in the world. When you know only 5 doctors of possibly thousands in the world, it is not a good statistical sample. If you must use the word best you should always qualify the statement by saying that for me he is the best.

Another word that we often use is picking up. You say that on my way home I will pick up milk or something. What you really mean is I am going to buy milk or something.

I have another friend who tells me that I talk a lot, which is incidentally true. Since I have traveled a lot I have a lot of interesting stories. I told him that what you can talk only about your kids, your home and your job, which is not that interesting to hear for anybody.

Accident is not a good word to me. One must know how to avoid getting into an accident. Why do we have speed limit posted in numbers? These speed limits are based on what are the chances of having an accident if you go above the recommended speed. We have statistical information to show that in the cities if you drive more than 35 miles/hour; there is a chance to have accident because there is a lot of slow moving traffic and also people walking and crossing roads. On the highway also, it is usually 55 mile/hr and this was decided so that chances of accidents are reduced and also we know that to get optimum mileage speed over 55miles/hr, one uses more gas. There is also a rule that you should not follow the car on the road in front of you at less than 10mph the speed of the car ahead. You should also not follow less than one car length. This is done so that if you have to brake all of a sudden you have time to react and stop the car before bumping into the car in the front of you.

Phrase 'see you later' does not mean he is really going to see you. In the beginning when somebody used that phrase I asked him, **When, When**?

Phrase 'back in a minute' does not mean really he will be back in sixty seconds. So whenever somebody asked me back in a minute, I always ask him or her how many seconds in your minute. Usually it should be 60 seconds, but it can be unto 1000 seconds or more, based on that person's definition of minute

Now days in India, the word actor applies to both the male and female gender. Just a couple of years back, the female actor was called Actress and male actor was called Actor. Now, however, women demand equality and do not want to be designated as actress. You can see that we are changing the words we use to signify more real situation. We know also now women do not want to be called Miss for unmarried and Mrs. for married. Now they are called Ms for both married and unmarried women.

My daughter started working for a company and she was given the firm's letter about taking your picture for records. The letter read that for pictures you must wear suit and a tie. She went to the personnel department and asked why you have written, suit and a tie. It is not correct, and she told him that you should change that wording so that it does not differentiate between men and women.

Dr. Vasant D. Chapnerkar

Words like awesome, mind blowing, and gorgeous cannot be quantified and hence give different meaning to different people.

Most of us use the term 'talking from the heart'. This is to show that you are not lying or fibbing. Actually I have mentioned before if you think from the heart then you are not doing the right thing. Heart is just a pump to blend air and blood and pumps it to different parts of the body. Heart does not have capacity to receive information and use it later. The brain does this work. So, how you can say that I am talking from the heart. People think that it is very important to use this term and they think it shows the real confidence in what they are saying.

We use words like love and hate. It does not mean anything to me. If you love somebody you spend more time with them, share your wealth and energy with them. So you can quantify love by time spent, money spent, and energy spent. When we were raising our kids and helping our kids raise grandkids, we spent time, money and energy so they could be good citizens of the world. If you hate somebody then you ignore them and do not spend the precious resources I call Time, Money and Energy.

Heartburn is another word does not really mean your heart is burning. It is really *acid reflux* caused by things, like spices, fruit juices, alcohol, and caffeine.

Stress is also caused by the words we use. If you say that distance to go is long, then you automatically are thinking it is bad. For person like me I do not use word long. It takes 24-30 hours to go to India from US. I call this short distance for me but most of the others it is too long. By using words like no, not, you are being negative and that causes stress. I rarely use such words. I have also do not have too much of a jet lag when I travel to India and back, because I change time on my watch and tell my brains *it is the time now where you are.*

PERORATION

Cliff Fadiman said, "A good memory is one trained to forget the trivial". "Living with the immediacy of death helps you sort out your priorities in life. It helps you to live a less trivial life." This is the profound message from Sogyal Rinpoche.

ಇಾ

Bibliography

http://www.brainyquote.com/quotes/keywords/statistics.html#Fd93ErVQoxwX7tS0.99

Chapter 7

Time

The best thing about the future is that it comes one day at a time.

Abraham Lincoln

Cଷ

Prime / Premiere . . .

"Time is the coin of your life. It is the only coin you have, and only you can determine how it will be spent. Be careful lest you let other people spend it for you."—Carl Sandburg

Time is *the most important thing in life*. Every one has 24 hours in a day. If you are a King you do not get any more or if you are an operator in a plant or any position does not get more or less than 24 hours. It is how you use this time that makes a difference between success and failure in life by what we consider standards.

It is always very difficult to decide the standards, because for some people, to have lot of economic assets is being successful and for some, to have the best health and for some, to have best education.

Why do they have PIP (Picture in Picture) in TVs? This way you can watch two shows during the time interval you use your PIP. I use PIP a lot to change from one channel to another if I want to watch two shows during any time period. You switch to the other channel if there is commercial on the first or what you are watching at that instant is not worth viewing.

Another thing, I do following three things in the same time period:

1. Make two cups of tea in the microwave (one for me and the other for my wife)
2. Perform my daily prayers
3. Perform physical exercise.

As mentioned earlier, I showed my granddaughter how to save time when checking out at the grocery store.

You have only 24 hours per day and if you lose time you cannot get it back, you cannot bank time either for using later like we do with the money resource.

During one of my trips, I experienced in Nepal, the balloon went up only on the day when we were there. The weather was not good before that. It was true on the recent trip to South Africa and India. It shows that the karma or what I call statistics was in my favor.

If you do not do what you want to do at the time you should do, then there is 90% chance that you will not do it. When you go to buy anything the seller tells you that I can give you all the discounts if you buy right now and it will not be available afterwards. He is doing that because he knows if you are not interested in buying now then chances of you coming to buy later are less than 10%.

To accumulate wealth you have to get other people working for you. There are not enough hours in a day for you to make money by yourselves. For a company to hire you you need to make at least 3 times the money they spend on you, otherwise they are losing money on you. You always have to figure out how much money you can make per unit hour. You make money only when you have people working for you. If you are a business person and you spend time doing cleaning or other chores which can be done by hiring labor and pay say $10 hour then you should assign those duties and pay $10 per and use that time to do your business and make many times $10. Bill Gates and all of the successful people make money by hiring other people to work for them. A doctor had his own practice and he decided to make more money, he hired many doctors to work for him and formed a company. He later started a health insurance company and sold it for a billion dollars. He could not have done it if he was just having his own practice.

Another thing we all do is—if you are caught in traffic with an accident ahead of you, you drive very slowly when your car comes to where there was accident so that you can satisfy your curiosity to see what happened. This is called **rubber necking**. What you are doing is, you are wasting your time and also of other people who are behind you.

You should do breathing exercises while you are driving or you are waiting to see someone.

Planning ahead will save time, money and energy. We always have options all the time to make the right decision. The decisions are always based on the pursuit of happiness. If you have a lot of money, then you do not worry about money, but try to maximize use of time and energy. If you are young and you have a lot of energy then you try to maximize use of money and time. If you are retired and do not have much to do with time, then you try to maximize use of money and energy.

When I was recently at the airport and was seeing signs to park my car for a one-day trip. I saw the sign said the remote parking will cost $ 6.95 and the parking at the terminal was $ 20.00. I had to make a quick decision where to park. I went through my thinking process and decided that I want to conserve my energy and time and decided to pay the higher fare to park my car in the terminal parking lot.

We always need to optimize energy, money and time usage. To conserve energy I always say that if you can sit, do not stand up, if you can lie down, do not sit.

When we plan, we also first make a 25-year plan and the objective of accomplishing the overall goal. Then with that in mind, you break your work into a first five-year plan and then you further break it in to one-year plan with defined activities and the action plan for each defined activity.

When I am traveling by car I always divide the journey into at least 3 parts. Say if you want to go from A to D, then I break that into from A to B, then from B to C and then from C to D. This way you feel that you are accomplishing your goal easily, because you do finish first part and you feel good about it, instead of thinking about the whole journey, which make you feel more tired and tense.

Both Time and Money are important in our lives. Of course I am assuming that health is not a factor in most decisions made between time and money. We always want the best of both, but it is not possible to have best of both and hence you have to make a good decision. We know sometimes there comes a point when you have to choose between having time for your family versus making more money. For each has to determine how much money is required to live at the standard you want to? It varies with age of the person making the decision. If you have young children, you want more time than money to raise them properly. When the kids are going to college, you will want more money and less personal time. In some cultures, the time is very important when your kids are less than 4 years old. It is very necessary that at least one of the parents should be there to take full care of children. In Indian culture the wife usually stays home or if the parents are living with them then it is all right. In American culture it is quite prevalent that both the parents work and keep the baby in nursery. People in day care without as much attention as parents would give rise what happens then is that the kids. This is the main reason why in Indian culture the divorce rate is 0.7 %, while in American culture it is 54.8%. The higher divorce rate also usually causes the children to get into trouble.

When you are raising kids, it is also necessary to use their time wisely. Some parents want them to be good in school and have many extracurricular activities, namely dancing, musical lessons, and clubs of various kinds and at the same time you want them to get A in all courses they take in school. You know what happens when your kids are forced into beauty contests they are made to grow up sooner than they should. We also know what has happened to Michael Jackson, mostly because of his parents made him just concentrate on music and never had any childhood. Hence, he was acting like a child in his thirties and forties.

When you are doing any job, you should be in the most comfortable position to accomplish that job in least amount of time. For instance, if you are on a ladder and want to tighten some screw, then you should be able to do it without twisting your body and worrying about falling down. If you position yourself, such that you have your body and hand in natural position, then the job is done in least time and you falling is avoided.

While traveling, use that time to organize your thoughts on something, which you have to do or write a letter or report.

When you have too many clothes and you don't use them for three years, then you need to give them to others, who are not privileged to have many clothes. You are making good use of your clothes that you will not use again. That is why we have Salvation Army, Purple Heart and other organizations that will come to your house and take those clothes and give them to the needy. When I mentioned clothes, it should not be limited to clothes only; things like shoes, appliances, TVs, and luggage are included.

When I go to India, I have a car with driver. Many times my driver used to go a longer route to avoid paying toll. He says why you want to pay money when you can save. I tell him that for me, if you save even 1 minute, I am willing to pay the toll. For his thinking, because he earns such a small amount of money, toll is a lot of money.

Even when you go to a restaurant, where you are a regular visitor and know their menu, you always decide what you are going to eat. You really in your mind number the priority of what you are going to eat. Again always, you assign no. 1 or no.2, for whatever you do and if no.1 is not available then you have already chosen no. 2. This saves you time to order and get your food sooner.

When you are going places, you always should plan your route in such a way that you do not back track. By not planning you can waste a lot of time, money and energy. This is particularly true now, that the price of gasoline is gone up so high. The recent statistics shows that people in US are driving more than 10 billion miles less now, than in the previous year.

PERORATION

'Time = Life, Therefore, waste your time and waste of your life, or master your time and master your life.'—Alan Lakein

৪০

Bibliography

http://www.brainyquote.com/quotes/keywords/statistics.html#Fd93ErVQoxwX7tS0.99

Chapter 8

Religion

"No one who does good work will ever come to a bad end, either here or in the world to come"

—*Anonymous, The Bhagavat Gita*

❧

Prime / Premiere . . .

This chapter is not to define religion or exalt the relative virtues of one over the other. I am not about to delve into any sermonizing either. It is neither a discussion on the philosophy of religion nor a theological discourse of any kind. I am writing this to underline the fact that many a myths, superstitions and beliefs prevail in the name of religion and umpteen undesirable activities are marketed under the guise of religious dictums. While one should be absolutely free to practice the faith one wishes to, it would help to be objective about one's beliefs and understand whether a practice has basis in science or religion or no basis at all.

We all have different faiths. We are a Hindu, a Muslim, a Christian, a Jew, or one of the many other faiths.

This all depends on our environment, surroundings, which gave us varied statistics to make our choice. All religions are, in essence, alike because they all advocate us to be good.

I have concluded that we say God does not want you to do the above things, because if we tell ignorant people that it is part of religion then they follow it blindly.

Every Tuesday **of the week**, I **do** choose not *to* eat meat, do not take alcoholic beverages and have only one meal. I do not do this to reduce my weight. I fast, in order to exercise power over my brain. ***Both of my*** daughters also started fasting on Tuesdays and additionally they stick to *a* vegetarian diet on Thursdays also. I have been doing this since 1983. Since I travel **a lot** to different countries with my clients, they always joke that they should take me to the best **of** the restaurants ***on Tuesday*** because I will not eat the expensive meat dishes on that day.

Since I was born to Indian parents, who were Hindus, I go to temples to worship; it is not to ask God to give me this or that. I go there to meditate and control my **base** *basic* desires in life. I get rid of bad thoughts and think of good things in life. We ***as humans*** also go to temples, churches, synagogues, and mosques to worship, because we know that every religion basically urges *us* to do good deeds.

When I was in Morocco, I visited the one of the most famous Mosques in the World. At the entrance, the attendant told me that if you are a Hindu, you couldn't enter the Mosque. **I do not think that** *For the most part* there is *not* a similar **problem** *issue* with respect to entering temples, churches or synagogues.

One of my goals in life was to visit all the countries in the World. Once I visited Pakistan. Since I am US citizen, I thought that I need not obtain a visa earlier, but would get a three-day visiting visa on reaching the country. Also, as it was a holiday in Delhi, India, I did not have the time to get a visa, so I went ahead to board the plane to Lahore, Pakistan. When I reached the airport and started going through immigrations, I was stopped and told that I could not enter the country, because I was an Indian. I showed him that I was a citizen of USA and hence could get visa at the airport. The immigration agent was very sorry that he could not let me enter because I was an Indian. He told me that if he were to let me enter, he would be in big trouble. Yet, since he felt bad for me he tried his best to get me in. I told him that a paper company named, Packaging Ltd, had invited me. I suggested that he could call the President of the company and see if he could come and stand as my guarantor. The company's President agreed and came and picked me up and took me to the hotel. At the hotel, an agent stood in front of my room to make sure that I would not escape. The next day the President of the company got me a three-day visa.

I was born on an auspicious day, Lord Krishna's birthday (the day is called Gokul Ashtami) and my son was born on a similar day in USA, which is Valentines' day. The Hindu mythology says that Lord Krishna performed *'ras-leela'* with *'gopikas'* (damsels who played with the Lord). This has analogy in the St. Valentine's Day—the day of expressing love in the western world.

We have many customs in Hindu religion, which have a bearing to general physiological well being than with faith. I could briefly, dwell upon a few.

Ekadashi: When we were growing up in the nineteen forties, adults usually fasted on the eleventh day (***Ek*** means 'one' and ***dashi*** means 'ten'), to clean up their system after eating normally for ten days. This was done to flush unwanted chemicals from the body (now you can do the same thing by taking laxatives and other such chemicals). As mentioned earlier, I do fast on every Tuesday, and all the people I know think that I do it as part of religion. But, it is not so. I do it to control my mind. It has a very positive effect.

At that time it was considered religious to not eat fish during and just after monsoon. The scientific reason was that bacteria were being washed into the sea and fish would eat them and then when you eat that fish you would get those bacteria in your body and eventually get sick. Now the fish are grown in fish hatcheries, where purified water is used and there is no reason to worry about eating bacteria when we eat fish.

Vaastu Shastra: It is the science of direction used by Indians. It says that when the house (mostly kitchen) faces in a particular direction, it brings bad luck. ***Vaastu Shanti*** is creating a congenial setting or a place to live or work, in a most scientific way, taking advantage of the benefits bestowed by the five elements called *'Panchamahabhootas'* 'pancha (the number 5), maha (big), bhootas (elements) of the nature thereby paving the way for enhanced health, wealth, prosperity and happiness in an enlightened environment.

Actually this has nothing to do with the facing of the house as a religious thing and there is no penalty for doing so. The facing of the house is based on the position of kitchen. It has to be facing west because the sun is hottest in the 2:00 pm to 4:00 pm period and if you have the kitchen facing the west it is hot. The kitchen should face the west so that one can do the cooking in the morning when the sun is facing east, the cooler time of the day.

Actually it is just a scientific situation. In olden times in India most of the women cooked in the morning and not having cooling fans, air conditioning or microwaves in those days, they did not want the Sun's rays to fall on the kitchen and make it uncomfortable to do the cooking. They also used wood and charcoal stoves, which gave out more heat to the surroundings. So they placed the kitchen in such a way that it got the evening sun and not the morning sun, to keep the kitchen and them cool. Microwaves we use now do not waste heat and hence does not make kitchens hot. So we can have the kitchen face any way we want.

It is said that the world comprises five basic elements. They are Earth, Water, Air, Fire and Space. Out of the nine planets, our planet has life because of the presence of theses five elements:

EARTH—the third planet, in order, from the sun, is a big magnet with North and South poles as centers of attraction. Its magnetic field and gravitational force has considerable effect on everything on the Earth, living and non-living.

WATER—This is represented by rain, river, and sea and is in the form of liquid, solid (ice) and gas (steam, cloud). It forms part of every plant and animal. Our blood is nothing but water with hemoglobin and oxygen.

AIR—As a life support element, air is very powerful life source. Human physical comfort values are directly and vitally dependent on correct humidity, airflow, temperature of air, air pressure and air composition.

FIRE—It represents light and heat without which the life will would not exist. All days and nights, seasons, energy, enthusiasm, passion, vigor is because of light and heat only.

SPACE—It is the shelter provider to all the above elements.

There is an invisible and constant relation between all the five elements. Thus the man can improve his conditions by properly designing his building by understanding the effectiveness of these five natural forces.

Most people in India wrongly feel that incorporating **Vaastu** principles in their premises require a lot of structural changes and this in turn makes them apprehensive, after all, making structural changes is expensive and at time not practical. However, this is a misconception as there are non-destructive remedies for any kind of **Vaastu** violation. Without breaking or demolishing anything, we can install certain remedial measures like pyramids, copper strips or plates to neutralize the negative forces. Our energy meter can measure its positive effect as well. An energy meter has been developed, which can detect the negative energy and properly identify the artifacts, plants in the garden that could be radiating negative energies and then help eliminating them.

Hindus should not eat Beef:

Another interesting belief that is quite prevalent especially in India is that Hindus should not eat beef; there is an ancient reason for this. Hindus consider that there are three things a child needs to survive and those are:

1. Sun
2. Water
3. Milk

For the above reasons, we worship the Sun, we worship the Sea and we worship the Cow, which gives milk.

In olden days it was thought that if you eat beef, you would have to kill the cow to get that meat. But, if you really think, we do not milk cows for the milk and then butcher them to get beef.

The cattle used for beef are not milking cows and hence we are not killing cows, which are considered as sacred in Hindu religion. Thus we are not taking away the source of milk for our consumption.

When I came to US in 1956, my guardians told I that I should not eat beef, because if you kill the cow it will not be able to give milk to the child. I tried not to eat beef and later found that most of the vegetables use beef broth in their cooking. In the US the cow is not used to provide milk and hence not eating beef does not hold.

In India the religion is used as a crutch, to tell ignorant people to do certain things because if you do not do those things God will be upset. I call these as plain scaring tactics.

In Indian philosophy, *ATMA* is Brain, *JIV* is Heart and *TAMAS* is Ignorance.

One way of looking is the three forms of thought, which the Hindus call Gunas also:

1. *Sattva gun*—pertaining to purity, thoughts that are pure and noble
2. *Rajas gun*—pertaining to passion, thoughts that are dipped in passion, are excited and agitated.
3. *Tamas gun*—pertaining to inertia, thoughts those are inert, dull or inactive.

We can compare the above with Intelligence, Stupidity and Ignorance.

Sattva or *Atma* is compared with Intelligence. *This type of person has a good brain and knows how to use the information stored in the brain and quickly gets the encoding, storing and decoding.* Statistically this person has the best chance of being successful in whatever he/she is doing.

Rajas or *JIV* is compared with Stupidity. *This type of person has information but does not know how to use it and causes problems.* I think because he is thinking from the heart. As I have said before heart does not have any information, it is just a pump to send blood to the brain. *Such a person does things out of passion, emotion and statistically is not able to act to resolve issues and achieve whatever he is trying to accomplish.*

Tamas—As mentioned earlier this relates to ignorance. This type of person does not have information and is called ignorant. This means he is not collecting a lot of statistically good information to make good decisions. *Such a person has a stereo-type life and does not travel much and normally does routine, menial jobs and has minimal chance to accomplish any other task than what he / she routinely does.*

The Chinmayanand Mission literature on Hinduism, defines Body, Mind, and Intellect. Atma controls these by Vasana and in turn, finally. They also talk about sub-conscience, conscience and super-conscience. They really are not any different, because they use the same statistical database stored in our brain. Based on this information one makes the decision what to do and what not to do. There is no other database that a person can get any information from. If you do not have enough of good information, then you naturally need to get more needed information and reach an optimum level to take right decisions in life.

I was attending a Hindu religious gathering. At this gathering a 69-year-old man asked the question that when I was in my teens, I wanted to be an Aeronautical Engineer, and I did not do it and was repenting that I always think about it. You have to have closure on any issue you deal with you; otherwise it is taking your good energy and turning into destructive energy. You always have to try what you want to do, as soon as you can, and if you cannot do it at that time you have to drop it.

I now wish to devote some part of this chapter to talk of the richness of Indian philosophy or way of life.

In the early phases of human life on this planet when man was struck with wonder or was amazed by the natural phenomena or when he found complex and conflicting phenomena in life and was filled with discontentment at the existing order of things, it was the beginning of philosophy.

The Vedas: The origin of Indian philosophy may be easily traced in the Vedas. The Vedas are the earliest available records of Indian literature. The Upanishads are the foundation of Indian philosophy, which teach spiritual monism and mysticism. The systems of Indian philosophy are systematic speculations on the nature of the Realty in harmony with the teachings of Upanishads, which contain various aspects of the truth. They aim at the knowledge of the Reality with a view to transforming and spiritualizing human life. Philosophical knowledge does not aim at merely satisfying our theoretical and speculative interest, but also at realizing the highest truth in life.

Dars'ana or visions of truth: Indian philosophy is intensely spiritual and emphasizes the need of practical realization of truth. As philosophy aims at knowledge of truth, it is termed in Indian literature, 'the vision of truth' (dars'ana). The word 'dars'ana' means 'vision' and also the 'instrument of vision'. It stands for the direct, immediate and intuitive vision of Reality, the actual perception of Truth, and also includes the means, which lead to this realization. 'See the Self' is the keynote of all schools of Indian Philosophy. And this is the reason why most of the schools of Indian Philosophy are intimately associated with religious sects.

The schools of Indian philosophy: The following are the major philosophical schools or systems (dars'anas).

1) The *Nyaya* system of *Aksapada Gautama*
2) The *Vaise esika* system of *Maharshi Kanada*
3) The *Samkhya* system of *Kapila Muni*
4) The *Yoga* system of *Patanjali*
5) The *Mimamsa* system of *Jaimini*
6) The *Vedanta* system of *Badarayana Vyas*
7) The *Bauddha* system of *Guatama Buddha*
8) The *Jaina* system of *Mahavira*
9) The *Charvaka* system of *Charvaka*

Classfication of the Indian Philosophical Schools:

Orthodox and Heterodox

The schools or systems of Indian philosophy are divided into two broad classes, namely, orthodox (astika, Vedic) and heterodox (nastika, Non-Vedic). To the first group belong the six chief philosophical systems (popularly known as ***sad-darsana***), namely, Mimamsa, Vedanta, Sankhya, Yoga, Nyaya and Vaisesika. These are regarded as orthodox (astika), not because they believe in God, but because they accept the authority of the Vedas. The Mimamsa and the Sankhya do not believe in God as the creator of the world, yet they are called orthodox (astika), because they believe in the authoritativeness of the Vedas. Under the other class of heterodox systems, the chief three are the schools of the Materialists like the Charvakas, the Bauddhas and the Jains. They are called heterodox because they do not believe in the authority of the Vedas.

Problems and Methods of Indian Philosophy: Though the basic problems of philosophy have been the same in the East as in the West and the chief solutions have striking similarities, yet the methods of philosophical enquiry differ in certain respects and the processes of the development of philosophical thought also vary. Indian philosophy discusses the various problems of Metaphysics, Ethics, Logic and Epistemology but generally it does not discuss them separately. The Indian philosopher from all possible approaches, metaphysical, ethical logical and epistemology discuss every problem. There are distinctions in the methods of speculation, adopted by different schools

Empiricism, Rationalism and Authoritarianism: The nine major systems of Indian Philosophy may be classified on the basis of sources of knowledge, i.e., epistemology into three major groups—Empiricism, Rationalism and Authoritarianism.

Empiricism: Those who hold that perception is the only source of knowledge are forced to deny the existence of God, soul, rebirth, hell and heaven. This view is called Empiricism—Sense experience is the only source of knowledge. ***Charvaka*** holds this view.

Rationalism: Those who hold that we are entitled to believe in what is not directly perceived but which can be inferred from what is perceived. This view is called Rationalism, for e.g., from the perception of smoke we are entitled to infer the existence of fire though we do not see fire, on the ground that wherever there is smoke there is fire. The Nyaya-Vaisheshika, the Samkhya-yoga and Buddhism are rationalist schools. They accept perception and inference as the valid ***pramanas*** and regard inference as primary and sense perception as subordinate.

Authoritarianism: Perception and Inference based upon perception may be adequate to give us knowledge about the empirical world, but what about transcendent realities like souls, God, past birth, karma hell and heaven. These objects are not knowable by these two *pramanas*. Yet they can be known through supra-sensuous experience of the mystics, prophets, saints, and seers directly and to us through scriptures, which are the records of such experience, or revelations this is called Authoritarianism. Of course, they accept other pramanas also. The remaining three schools of purva Mimamsa, Vedanta and Jainism belong to this category.

Common Ideas in the System of Indian Philosophy

i) *The Reality of the world*: All schools of Indian philosophy recognize the reality of the world. Even the Advaita Vedanta of Samkara regards the world as a mere appearance from the standpoint of the absolute. But it recognizes the empirical reality of the world-appearance.

ii) *The reality of the self*: The reality of the permanent self is generally admitted. Among the heterodox schools the Charvaka and Buddhist deny the reality of the permanent self.

iii) *The law of Karma*: All schools of Indian philosophy except the Charvaka believe in the law of Karma. As we sow, so we reap. There is no escape from the consequences of actions. Their fruits must be reaped in this life or in a future life

iii) *Transmigration*: The idea of transmigration is common to all systems of Indian philosophy except the Charvaka school.

iv) *Initial Pessimism and Ultimate Optimism*: Indian philosophy is branded as pessimistic. Life is full of sufferings. But all kinds of pain can be destroyed in the state of liberation. So, Indian philosophy is characterized by initial pessimism and ultimate optimism.

v) *Bondage*: Another common view held by all Indian thinkers except Charvaka School, is that ignorance of reality is the cause of our bondage and sufferings, and liberation from these cannot be achieved without knowledge of reality.

vi) ***Liberation***: The idea of liberation is common to all the systems of Indian philosophy except the Charvaka School.

vii) ***The means to liberation***: The different systems of Indian philosophy lay down the means to the attainment of liberation.

viii) ***Pramanas***: Indian philosophy is not dogmatic. Every system of philosophy is based on epistemology or theory of knowledge.

PERORATION

As I move further on, it would be pertinent to underscore that while charlatans all along history have manipulated and misused the name of religion to propagate ideas and practices having no real roots anywhere except in vested interests, there have been benevolent souls too, who have used religion to inculcate, in ordinary and ignorant people, simple ideas pertaining to humanity or human life rather than to divinity, for example, the maxim, 'Cleanliness is next to godliness' itself has basis in this benign approach. I am not a particularly religious person but I do believe that for the larger good of humanity, if some scientific facts are followed by common men in the belief that it is a religious good, then no harm is being caused to any one. This is akin to worshipping a stone sculpture taking it as an image of a deity and vice versa not worshipping a deity because it is nothing but stone.

What is important is not the religion or the faith but the philosophy of humanity. Hence I have briefly dwelt upon it, giving the readers a fleeting insight into the right values that were the basis of Indian philosophy and way of life.

৵

Bibliography

1. Quote from Bhagvat Gita
    http://www.goodreads.com/work/quotes/1492580-bhagavad-gita
    Accessed: 13.1.25

Chapter 9

Our Body & Mind

We can make a commitment to promote vegetables and fruits and whole grains on every part of every menu. We can make portion sizes smaller and emphasize quality over quantity. And we can help create a culture—imagine this—where our kids ask for healthy options instead of resisting them.

Michelle Obama

Cℛ

Prime / Premiere . . .

We have so got carried away with our inner voice that we have started thinking that thinking about our body is of secondary importance and what is important is how our inner self is or that we can always think about the body later, after all it is not running away. We do this till one day the body packs up and raises it's hands saying, "Boss, I can't go any further". It is only then that we reluctantly start paying attention to it. How wrong indeed are acting and we thinking?

Deepak Chopra says that the way you think, the way you behave, the way you eat, can influence your life by 30 to 50 years. Yet we gamble with it. We take it for granted almost presuming that it's body's duty to take care of it and us as well. I hope the following chapter will catalyze some change.

What do we mean by BODY?

It can be seen. It is physical, being made of various materials. It has many parts and organs; to name a few—it has arms, legs, spine, and many joints like—ankle, knee, hip, elbow, and shoulder. It consists of organs like heart, lungs, brain, colon, pancreas, liver, intestines, muscles, and veins.

What do we mean by MIND?

When we want to talk about mind, it has several meanings and we need to be clear about them before we talk about it.

The **human brain** is a part of the body that plays a very important role in our life. It is like computer hardware. It is the center of the human nervous system and a highly complex organ. It monitors and regulates the body's actions and reactions. It continuously receives sensory information and rapidly analyzes this data and then responds, controlling bodily actions and functions. The neo-cortex is the center of higher-order thinking, learning and memory. The cerebellum is responsible for the body's balance, posture and the coordination of movement.

In spite of the fact that the thick bones of the skull protect it, suspended in cerebrospinal fluid and isolated from the bloodstream by blood-brain barrier, the delicate nature of the human brain makes it susceptible to numerous types of damage and diseases. The most common forms of physical damage are closed head injuries such as a blow to the head, a stroke, or poisoning caused by a wide variety of chemicals that can act as neurotoxins. Infection of the brain is rare because of the barriers that protect it, but is very serious when it occurs. The human brain is also susceptible to degenerative disorders, such as Parkinson's disease, multiple sclerosis and Alzheimer's disease. A number of psychiatric conditions, such as schizophrenia and depression, are widely thought to be caused at least partially by brain dysfunctions, although the nature of such brain anomalies is not well understood.

Brain scan takes a look inside the growing Brain. What brain changes transform children from creatures of impulse into fully functioning adults? In a 2001 study that used MRI imaging, researchers at the University of Pittsburgh identified the key brain changes that signal mental maturity.

How and where the brain changes? Once a child hits adolescence, the brain having mastered basic cognitive abilities, no longer grows in size. The adolescent years are a flurry of complex reorganization as the brain decides what's needed, what's unnecessary, and how to achieve maximal efficiency.

Adolescent brains undergo synaptic pruning, in which more useful neural connections are nourished while lesser important connections wither away. Nipping unnecessary synapses in the bud actual leads to deactivation in many regions as the growing brain sheds excess neural activity like baby fat. At the same time, the brain begins to active regions such as the **prefrontal cortex** that handle abstract cognitive abilities. Of these abilities, **impulse control** is a key in attaining adult-level mental maturity.

MRIs reveal where impulse control takes place. Researchers have used MRI brain scans to compare brain activation in 254 subjects as they performed an **antisaccade task.** These subjects were divided into children (ages 8-13), adolescents (14-17) and adults (18-30). Adults performed the best and children the worst, but more interesting is how their differences manifested.

The **antisaccade** task measures impulse control by tracking subjects' **saccades,** or eye movements. As subjects stare at a blank screen, a light flashes briefly. The goal is to look in the opposite direction from the light. This simple premise is a complex task—and, for untrained brains, an effortless one. It requires superior impulse control to both keep task goals in mind and resists the instinct to look.

Children, who made many errors, largely activated the brain's **supramarginal gyrus.** This may indicate that children relied more on visual cues to compensate for other immature brain processes.

Adolescents, in contrast, activated the **prefrontal cortex** more than other groups. Activity in this area, which manages **working memory** and **executive control,** evinces brains beginning to maintain higher-level plans and goals.

Adult brains showed the widest pattern of brain activity, lighting up over 5 different brain regions. This is strong evidence that the ability to voluntarily start and stop behavior—to plan rather than merely react—is a mature product of the synaptic pruning and organization that happens in adolescence. The adult brain is an efficient engine, quickly processing varied information to form a cohesive strategy.

Luckily research has found that you can optimize crucial adult abilities well past adolescence. By shaping new neural patterns, various exercises have been shown to improve working memory and executive control.

The **mind** is the aspect of intellect and consciousness experienced as a combination of thought, perception, memory, emotion, will and imagination, to the thought processes of reason. Mind manifests itself subjectively in a stream of consciousness. In popular usage **mind** is frequently synonymous with thought: the private conversation with ourselves that we carry on "inside our heads." Thus we "make up our minds," "change our minds," or are "of two minds" about something. One of the key attributes of the mind in this sense is that it is a private sphere to which no one but the owner has access. No one else can "know our mind." They can only try to interpret what we consciously or unconsciously communicate.

The **intelligence** is an umbrella term describing a property of the mind including related abilities, such as the capacities for problem solving. The theory of intelligence is two-fold:

(i) the 'single intelligence' based upon the unilinear construct of "general intelligence",
(ii) The construct of multiple intelligences.

Intelligence is a true, biologically based mental faculty that can be studied by measuring a person's reaction times to cognitive tasks.

The **soul** is the incorporeal essence of a person or living thing. The soul has often been deemed as integral or essential to consciousness and personality, and may be synonymous with spirit, mind or self.

Atma is a philosophical term used in Hinduism, especially in the Hindu scriptures, to identify the soul whether in global sense or in individual sense. It is one's true self beyond identification with the phenomenal reality of worldly existence.

So while we are living, we must have our body functioning to keep all systems working, for when the soul leaves the human being is dead.

The human body is designed to generate all the chemicals needed by the body to function properly. We can do this by eating the right foods and not causing environmental degradation.

Our body is really a chemical factory. Our body is supposed to produce all the chemicals we need to lead a useful life. To enable it to do this, we have to eat well and exercise well. As mentioned earlier, we know that people who live in the mountains and even aborigines do not go to doctors, dentists, and optometrists and still live for 125 years. They do not have two things, which we have to deal with *viz.* tension and pollution.

We, the average, normal human beings living on this earth have these two big problems—stress and pollution. Stress is a technical word indicating a kind of restriction of flow of blood.

To avoid stress you need to have good information to make any decision. In my case I complete my tasks mostly because I use the statistical information to know which path to take and which path not to take to accomplish my task. I always have at least two choices as the first and the second option. When a person takes up a task and he is not successful in accomplishing it, he gets stressed out and cannot even think about the other alternative because he is in a stressed up state and cannot think properly.

On May 20ᵗʰ, 2012, Tampa Tribune had following editorial:

What is it with these surveys? And why don't people like us?

If there is a quality-of-life survey out there, you can be rest assured that Tampa is going to be at or near the bottom. It could be health-care or education or even attendance at baseball games. We are going to end up the cellar-dwellers of the list.

It was back in January 2012, when a national survey listed Tampa as the most stressed-out city in America. (Though I live in Tampa, I have stress-free life style).

Now granted, that it was around the time, when we still were wondering what had happened to our football team and were beginning to realize the Republicans and thousands of unhappy protesters were coming our way in August 2012, but was that enough to make us the most stressed-out city around?

You wonder if those surveyors ever tried to negotiate their way through downtown Atlanta at rush hour, been caught by accident in the wrong part of St. Louis after dark or maybe even been in Detroit at any time of the day. Had they tried going to the beach in Cleveland or getting a decent Cuban sandwich in Duluth, Minnesota?

So now along comes something known as the "Credibility Consumer Stress Index". I never heard of the thing and right away you have to wonder if someone is misspelling 'credibility'.

All I know is that in this index, we (Tampa, Florida WHO IS WE?) are at the top of the financial stress list, which is not a good thing. No.2 is Detroit, followed by Miami/Fort Lauderdale. It claims to be an index that measures quarterly shifts in the financial condition of average households. Right away there is a problem. You tell me what passes for an "average" household any more and if a Tampa family is any more or less average one in, say, Ohio or Utah.

"Unemployment is high and underemployment is also high", said a spokesman for the index about life around here. He adds, "13.2 percent of the houses are delinquent on their mortgages."

In the third quarter of 2007, Tampa's job market was at its strength with a score of better than 90 on the index. Since then, that score has dropped 40 point from a "secure" market to a "crisis" market, cased by the banks giving loans freely, without checking whether the household can afford to pay the mortgage payments.

May be there is some truth to theses surveys. Like most places, elsewhere in the country, we are caught up in a lingering and painful recession.

A blue-collar town likes this with average wages at best and an economy heavily dependent on real estate, there is no question we are hurting but surveys do not measure everything. Tampa is also a city of neighborhoods. It is a town where we reach out and do what we can. I have been writing about the genuinely caring people and organizations around here long enough to know we are also a city that comes together when it has to.

Are we stressed out financially? Around our house, the Bank of Otto has seen better days, and I do not have to look too far around our neighborhood, to see real crises. But I also see neighbors looking after each other and working hard to make things better.

To be free of stress, some people join a laughing club. Most of the yoga teachers also recommend laughing freely. Usually in a yoga class laughing is done very loudly. Indian physician, Dr. Madan Kataria in Mumbai in 1995, started the first laughing club. Today, the Laughter Movement has spread widely and is well accepted. It has become a global phenomenon with over 6000 clubs in 60 countries. Realizing the tremendous power of laughter, its efficacy and putting it into practice is the best prescription for wellness. Laughter Clubs have brought smiles and laughter in the lives of many people suffering from physical, mental and emotional upsets.

Laughter is the best medicine. Humor is infectious. When laughter is shared, it binds people together and increases happiness and intimacy. Laughter also triggers healthy physical changes in the body. Humor and laughter strengthen your immune system, boost your energy, diminish pain, and protect you from the damaging effects of stress. Nothing works faster or more dependably to bring your mind and body back into a balance than a good laugh. Humor lightens your burdens, inspires hope, connects you to others, and keeps you grounded, focused and alert.

To summarize:

1. Laughter is good for your health. It relaxes the whole body. A good, hearty laugh relives physical tension and stress, leaving your muscles relaxed for up to 45 mines after.
2. Laughter boosts the immune system. Laughter decreases stress hormones and increases immune cells and infection-fighting antibodies, thus improving your resistance to disease.
3. Laughter triggers the release of endorphins, the body's natural feel-good chemicals. Endorphins promote an overall sense of well being and can even temporarily relive pain.
4. Laughter protects the heart. Laughter improves the function of blood vessels and increases blood flow, which can help protect you against a heart attack and other cardiovascular problems.

I have my way of bringing laughter to people. At the end of any conversation on the phone, the party talking to you asks you "What else can I do for you?" When I hear that, I always tell, "I want you to deliver one million dollars in one dollar bills", and then I always get a laugh. To get one more laugh, I tell them that I am in good mood, so you keep the first one million dollars and send me the second one. I then get another laugh.

We talk about stress and tension. These are technical terms that indicate a kind of restriction of flow of blood. Why does this happen? When you are tense the cross sections of the veins, which carry blood, reduce in size and hence now the hearts need to push blood at high pressure causing a higher blood pressure. You can see this phenomenon also when you are in water and you get stressed the air from the body is removed and hence your body density overall goes up and the person sinks. Normally when you are relaxed and swimming your body has a lot of air, the density of which is only 0.6 gm/cc, while the density of your body fat is 1.4 gm/cc. The total density is determined by weight averaging the density of all the material in the body. When the air is there it is low and when air is removed, it goes up and hence you sink.

When we take any medicine, it is one particular chemical in it that we need to use to correct the system, since the body is not able to produce that chemical under the prevailing conditions. In this situation, we are also getting some other chemicals, which produce other effects, and usually they are not desirable. We call these as side effects of that particular medicine. We always see on the TV when they advertise that particular medicine they devote more time on the side effects of that medicine than talk about the effectiveness of that medicine.

To maintain a good, healthy body one should eat properly and exercise, but to maintain a good mind one needs to do yoga and meditation. Meditation calms our mind. Yoga helps prevent any health problems, by breathing better and excising the right parts of the body. When we breathe properly, we take in oxygen from the air we breathe. This oxygen goes to all parts of the body, especially to the brain. Using oxygen from the air the body burns food (mostly carbohydrates) and produces calories and an exhaust of carbon dioxide, which is bad for your health.

It is really strange that we see advertisements on TV by drug companies talking about their prescription medicines and asking us to tell our doctor to prescribe that for us. I thought that is what the doctors are for. The Doctors are supposed to know whether we need that medicine or not and they should prescribe. USA and New Zealand are the only two countries in the World that advertise prescription drugs on TV.

Dr. Vasant D. Chapnerkar

In the book, **_Freakonomics_** there is quite a comprehensive discourse on how medicines are approved or not approved by the F.D.A. (Federal Drug Administration). This book claims that it is very partial in its way of approving medicines for use. They claim that natural medicines (Ayurvedic or Homeopathic medicines) are not approved by FDA. They claim that there is a lot of politics in this process. We all know that the patents for drugs are issued and are valid for 17 years before anybody else can manufacture that medicine. If you think about it, it takes many years and billions of dollars to get the prescription medicines approved by FDA. So I guess they need to charge the extra price, yet these prices are exorbitant and drug companies make a lot of profit that can't be truly justified. Now days, many drug companies are offering these medicines at discounted prices for needy people, who otherwise wouldn't be able to afford them.

Antidepressants are good for avoiding fast decline due to Alzheimer. It is now recognized that drinking red wine, a glass a day, makes you have less chance of having a heart attack. Same is true about taking 85mg aspirin tablet per day. When I was growing up in Bombay my mother used to drink Red wine (Ruby Port) and hence when I came to this country in 1956 I started drinking red wine, one glass a day to this day I am having it.

Now it is reported quite often that if you use turmeric, ginger, garlic in your cooking and eat walnuts, and pistachios, you have a better chance to be healthier. By the same token, drinking soft drinks is bad for your health because it has preservative and many other additives, which are not good for your health.

To make a good impression on the person you are talking to, it is good if you stand erect and have head up. In Indian culture to get blessing from elders and Gods we always bow our head to admit their superiority.

When I had my knee replacement surgery, I was miserable for three days, when I gained some strength I told my brain that body had taken over until now and you better take the control back . . .

PERORATION

Our Vedas and Shashtras have in innumerable ways said that the human body is a palace created for the soul to dwell. We must guard and preserve the palace in order to take care of the soul, at the same time never to give importance to the body over the real inner spirit, the soul for one day it is bound to perish. We must do our best to keep it in good condition—working and efficiently completing all its expected tasks.

Jivaraj was the personal physician and surgeon of Gautam Buddha. He dedicated himself completely to health and well being of Buddha and other Monks. Occasionally, he also attended to others under instruction or permission from Gautam. His knowledge and ability ranged from curing infections to performing surgeries . . .

. . . This was 2,500 years ago and people reached out to him to keep their health and body in good condition. In the modern age, with a million advanced diagnostic tools and specialties and super-specialties at our service and fastest and latest research statistical data available on the various ailments and their cures, if we still ignore our health, whom else should we hold responsible but ourselves.

ॐ

Bibliography

http://www.brainyquote.com/quotes/topics/topic_health.html

Chapter 10

Longevity

Ayurveda is a sister philosophy to yoga. It is the science of life or longevity and it teaches about the power and the cycles of nature, as well as the elements.

Christy Turlington

∞

Prime / Premiere . . .

Cat Cora said, "I believe that parents need to make nutrition education a priority in their home environment. It's crucial for good health and longevity to instill in your children sound eating habits from an early age."

We know that it takes several billion dollars to get a drug approved by FDA. Hence, the drug companies are given 17 years during which no generic drug can be marketed. We also know that countries like India and China manufacture similar drugs and sell them for about 25% of the price in USA. They can do that because they do not have to recover the money USA has to spend to get the drug approved. It is also true of any patent, which has a life of 17 years before anyone else can use this finding. We also know that there is no enforcement procedure to stop other countries from using that finding.

Life Cycle:

Graph showing how age affects you, and how you can do normal things like walking, running, eating, seeing, hearing, and breathing.

When the child is born he does very few things, we teach him to eat, crawl, and walk. When he gets around the age 20-30 he is able to do the most with any activities (I assume that is 100 % effectiveness). The child at birth starts with 0% effectiveness.

Then after 30 years we all start losing some of the effectiveness. I assume at the following ages what the efficiencies are (these are not exact numbers).

You can consider that your heart beats at 80 beats /minute and every year it is flexing 42,048,000 times and if you live for 100 years it would have flexed 4,204,800,000 times. You multiply your heart beats/min multiply by 1440 minutes/day multiply by 365 days / year and multiply by your age in years. Based on this analysis and since my heartbeat now is 90/min, my heart has been beating for 47,304,000—times every year. For you to survive, you have to have your heart beat all the time and cannot stop even for one beat.

You know that if you use elastic band in your shorts after using that for may be few times (I suspect, it may be 500 times) it does not flex anymore. Scientists call this hysterics. So you can see how the heart wears off.

You can also think the same about all your joints, which flex so many times and hence as you get older the heart and the joints need repair or replacement. The progress made now in keeping heart and joints in use longer than before is based on the statistical information we collected to warrant more research.

It is interesting to note that people who collect old cars, they usually refurbish the old car to look and drive like new, by using replacement parts viz. tires, engine, seats, and paint. We should be able to do that to the human body and make it live for more than 100 years. We know that the people in the mountains live normally about 124 years. This is because they have clean environment and also eat right food so that the body can produce all the chemicals the body needs to live longer. We, on earth, have two major problems:

- Is that we breath air which contains 21% oxygen, which we need, we also get carbon dioxide, carbon monoxide, sulphur oxides, all of which are all harmful to the body.
- Is that when your body does not produce the chemicals we need to exist, hence we take medication for a particular chemical deficiency. When we do that we also get several other chemicals, which may be harmful for your longevity. You see the advertisement TV or in print that all the manufacturers of medicines always mention the side effects of taking their particular medicine.

Table II: AGE VERSUS % LIFE EFFECTIVENESS

Conditions	Age	Efficiency	Special
Just Born	0		
	20-30	100	Good Health
	40	60	Cannot run
			Start using bifocal lenses
	50	50	Cannot walk miles
	60	40	Need cataract surgery
	65	35	Need hearing aid
	70	30	Bones break, usually while taking a bath
	75	25	Need a knee replacement, start using Depends
	80	20	Need a hip replacement
	85	15	Cannot see, hear or walk well
	90	10	No energy to do physical activity, cannot sleep
	100	0	You are finished.

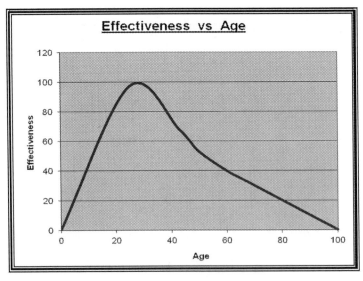

Figure 5

Based on the chart (Table II) the Figure 5 shows graphically the effectiveness vs. age. We could make a sheet to score for each person and find out how he does with what we all call normal for that age.

Assign 1 to 10 points for all the things you can do based on the chart. If you have very bad sight, we can assign 1-2 points and if your eyesight is 20/20 we can assign 10. If you add up the score for all the things mentioned, then you get the total score for you at the age you are able to find out what your problems are to achieve high marks.

Every person or object has a life cycle.

Every product made has its own life cycle:

When you are developing a new product for the market, then the life cycle of that product depends on who is in charge. In the beginning, the Research and Development has to be in driver's seat because they have to be able to produce product that is economically viable as against what is available in the market. When the market gets saturated with similar products from other companies, then it is time for the marketing people to convince the buyer that their product is superior to competition and hence they are in control. When the product is nearing obsolescence then it is again goes to the Research and development. They are again in charge to produce a product, which is better than the competition. And the cycle goes on.

The strategy to introduce a new product depends on the market evaluation by the marketing people so that R & D can give them a product better than their competition to sell.

It is interesting to note that VCR was (**first**) developed in U S and (**yet**) Japan capitalized on it and marketed VCR first. Xerox designed even the computer mouse and the computer itself but they did not market it. We all know the Xerox story, Mr. Chester Floyd Carlson developed Xerox copying technique and tried to sell it to IBM and other big companies, but they told him that it would not work. Then a small company named Haloid Corporation bought it for a very low price. In fact it is claimed that most of the Xerox employees made more money from Xerox Corporation than the person who invented the process, Mr. Carlson.

We also know that Mr. Deming, an American, went to all automobile companies in US and asked them to build quality cars, which can last longer. No one listened to him and said that we do not want the strategy of building long lasting cars, because we want the public to buy cars every two years and hence we should not build permanence in our design of car. We know now what happened as a consequence, because you see Toyota, Nissan, Honda and other foreign cars captured automobile market. Today, Toyota claims that they are the biggest producer of cars in the world by taking over that honor from General Motors. I remember Datsun (now Nissan) cars were manufacturing the same model for more than ten years. But at that time Americans did not prefer small cars because the cost of gasoline till 1974 was only $0.33/ gallon.

Ford also introduced a small car, called Pinto and GM introduced a small car, called Chevette and both did not make it in the long run. Since the quality was not as good as foreign cars it did not last long. Toyota has been marketing Corolla and Camry for ages. But now this fever of marketing new cars every year has caught on by the foreign car manufacturers also.

When the competition from foreign cars became too much for local manufacturers, they invited Dr. Deming and Ford is now using their slogan "*Quality is No. 1*".

When Airbus (a joint British—French venture) decided to build the plane for the future they decided to build a big plane, which can hold more than 500 passengers. The plane was called Airbus 380. But Boeing decided not to go that route but build more fuel-efficient plane, which can accommodate up to 400 passengers. The plane was called Boeing 787. The present situation is that Airbus 380 is way behind schedule and most think that to handle that many passengers will not be possible for most airports in the world and hence their orders are down. While Boeing is very happy with their strategy of building fuel-efficient plane and have many orders that will come on stream soon.

LCD, LED and Plasma technologies have revolutionized TV. Sony, a major manufacturer of TV decided to go with LCD, LED technology and did not develop Plasma technology. The LCD TVs are almost the same quality of picture as Plasma and cost only half as much. Of course the advantage of Plasma is that it can be mounted on the wall.

According to old information, we always said that after 40 years, he is over the hill, meaning that whatever was expected out of his life, if he had not attained by 40, the chances of him doing that later, is very less. However, since now the people are living longer because of good medical advances, this over the hill is now 50 may be even 60 years . . .

I have many of my friends and relatives who have died in their early sixties because I believe they did not accomplish their goals in life. All of them have died of heart attack. So now, exercising and not gaining too much weight is highly recommended and eating more vegetarian food.

PERORATION

Aaliyah said, "I think it's important to take a break, you know, from the public eye for a while, and give people a chance to miss you. I want longevity. I don't want to get out there and run myself ragged and spread myself thin." This should sum up both the material and philosophical need for longevity, which we all crave . . .

ો

Bibliography

Http://www.brainyquote.com